Natural or Supernatural?

Natural or Supernatural?

A Casebook of True, Unexplained Mysteries

Martin S. Caidin

CB

CONTEMPORARY
BOOKS

CHICAGO

Library of Congress Cataloging-in-Publication Data

Caidin, Martin, 1927–
    Natural or supernatural : a casebook of true unexplained
mysteries / Martin Caidin.
        p.   cm.
    ISBN 0-8092-3804-7 (paper)
    1. Science—Miscellanea.   2. Unidentified flying objects.
3. Curiosities and wonders.   4. Supernatural.   I. Title.
Q173.C12   1993
001.9′4—dc20   93-12972
                                                                    CIP

CONTENTS

Preface   vii

1   "My Name Is Smith and I'm from Anywhere"   1

2   Where Did They Come from and Where Do They Go?   23

3   The Great UFO Circus   41

4   "A Terrifying Sight"   69

5   It's All in the Perception   79

6   Who Cares If It's Not Real? It Works!   103

7   Monster Myth, Monster Reality   119

8   Living Memories and Old Friends   145

9   Prophecy for Apollo   167

10   That Damned Trapezium   175

11   "Nothing Will Help—He's Dead"   199

PREFACE

Ours is a world of scientific marvels, engineering wonders, and technological miracles. Our accomplishments enable us to cross an ocean in a few hours, watch astronauts walking on the moon, peer into the volcanoes of Mars and the moons of Jupiter, and watch films of exploring vessels nearly seven miles beneath the surface of the ocean. We have sent the first robot spacecraft on their way out of our solar system, perhaps to reach other worlds a million or ten million years from now. We scan the heavens with massive banks of super radio telescopes hoping to eavesdrop on signals from other civilizations thousands of light-years from our own world. We communicate planet-wide in seconds, we enable the deaf to hear, and the crippled to walk, and we transplant human organs with ease. We have sundered the atom, pondered the interior of the sun, and traced the paths of electrical currents through billions of connections in the brain.

But we do not know what lurks in the dark forests just beyond our homes.

Year after year, as science advanced and technology spun shining new webs in an ever more industrial world, the engineers and technicians who led the way promised us that science would banish myth and superstition. They would provide us with answers to the questions that had confounded, dumbfounded, amazed, and frightened men and women for centuries. No longer would we have to believe that lightning was hurled by invisible but powerful gods in an unreachable heaven. They would put to rest the

vii

notion that rocks fell from the sky. They would banish forever the tales of hairy creatures scrambling through dense brush and dark forests. And they would eliminate once and for all the nonsensical ideas that human beings could communicate with their minds, that they could die but not die, that spirits and nonhuman beings shared this world with us.

In short, in this era of huge engines, powerful machines, tall buildings, enormous ocean liners, great winged aircraft, microscopes, and telescopes, we would be free of the hauntings of our past lives. Wonder and enchantment, belief in magic and astrological forecasts, faith in dreams . . . all these must give way to scientific explanation and be banished forever from the planet. Science promised us a neat, orderly, and explainable world. In this new age of science, technology, computers, and other marvelous devices, superstition would belong only to those who refused to listen.

Fortunately, some of us still believe in mystery and enchantment. We *know* in our minds and hearts that the wonders of the world cannot be reduced to lifeless numbers and formulas. It has turned out that the great engines of science and technology often have the bad habit of spinning their wheels uselessly. The more we learn, the more questions we seem to raise.

Perhaps the greatest problem is that science cannot explain what *supernatural* really means. For example, among the most publicized of all mysteries has been the strange objects that race about the world, fly thousands of miles an hour, and are reported to have landed on the earth by thousands of people. The term *UFO* has become part of our everyday language, and we seem to be as much at a loss now to understand these strange objects as were the astonished onlookers of ancient times.

But while UFOs have captured headlines as well as attention, they remain just one part of a world filled with wonder and mystery. Science told us that the last great frontier was outer space, and we have accomplished great deeds in exploring space. No longer do we wonder what the outer planets (with the exception of Pluto) are like because we have thousands of photographs of these distant worlds. How strange, then, that we know more about conditions on our moon, and even on Mars and Venus, than we do about the deep ocean bottoms of our own planet. We still encounter weird creatures, we find life where we believe none could exist, and we *still* search for one of the greatest ancient mysteries—dazzling Atlantis, which both frustrates us and invites us to continue searching for a world lost in time.

There is little question that an even greater frontier is now being explored—the depths of the human mind. The abilities of human beings to perform feats once considered impossible or mythological have become fact. The new wave of parapsychology proves that mysteries, no matter how farfetched they seem to be, must be neither dismissed nor accepted without extensive research and a gradual accumulation of data.

For centuries arguments have raged about the so-called water witches—people who use divining rods of wood, metal, or other materials to find water concealed far beneath the ground. Science insists there is no proof that dowsing for water has any substantial basis, but dowsers keep right on finding not only hidden water, but metal and structures placed deep within the earth. The practice of dowsing rose to new heights when, during the Vietnam War, hard-bitten and pragmatic Marine Corps combat veterans made dowsing part of their regular combat training protocol and proved—in battle—that dowsing could help them find concealed enemy tunnels and weapons.

We are still beleaguered by poltergeists. These "noisy ghosts" have coexisted with us for thousands of years. They throw dishes and other objects around a home. They set furniture ablaze. The invisible and inexplicable poltergeists often hurl a barrage of stones at buildings, smashing windows, walls, and rooftops. Such events have been witnessed by thousands of people, many of them police officers, scientists, and men and women of high repute. What causes these frenzied outbursts of physical action? Scientists prefer not to respond to questions about such events because they have no answers except disbelief—which is the same as branding thousands of reliable witnesses as either liars or crazy. Again, this is a field where we are chasing . . . we know not what.

For hundreds of years people throughout the world have sworn to have seen and sometimes encountered huge man-beasts that have no niche in the scientific nomenclature of terrestrial life. Early Europeans spoke of great black killer dogs and werewolves and vampires. Superstition ruled our lives for hundreds of years, and ours was a world of faeries, trolls, troglodytes, and witches who could change from human to animal form and back again. There were demons and angels, winged humans, goblins, and dragons. Now, with our ability to communicate between any part of the world and another, we are dumbfounded to discover that great beasts, apelike creatures called Sasquatch and Bigfoot and other names, are still reported by thousands of people all over this planet. Animals have been seen that scientists insist cannot exist. People have heard them scream, seen them run. Some have been attacked by these creatures, and the creatures themselves have been shot and attacked in turn by terrified people. Where do they come from? How do they continue to defy discovery? How do they manage to survive in a world where civilization encroaches on all natural space? We lack answers to these questions, but of one thing we are certain—they are still as frightening and mysterious as ever.

The goblins and trolls of ancient times seem reluctant to disappear from the modern world, for people still encounter creatures of small stature with glowing eyes and strange powers—little demonic beings that terrify humans and animals alike with their sudden appearances and their ability to vanish at will.

More and more scientists are stepping across the line to a concept that once seemed fanciful and incredible—that perhaps the everyday life we know so well exists side by side with other dimensions. Visitation between worlds and times would explain many of the mysteries that still fascinate and plague us.

There are too many cases of people seemingly being displaced into the past, and other folk from the past being thrust suddenly and mysteriously into the future. History has many tales of people from ancient times appearing suddenly in the present, just as people among us—hundreds every year, if the police reports are true—vanish suddenly, sometimes before the very eyes of stunned witnesses. Sometimes they never return, but sometimes they do, with fascinating details of what they encountered that could *only* be explained by inadvertent "time travel."

Even in areas of land and ocean that are intimately familiar to us, we are baffled by the unexplained disappearances of airplanes and ships with all the people aboard them—never to be seen again, leaving not the slightest shred of wreckage or evidence that they ever existed. We are trying desperately to understand the "strange forces" that prevail in such areas as the feared Bermuda Triangle, which covers a large area of the ocean east of the United States. It is not natural for magnetic compasses to spin wildly and without warning or reason. It is not natural for gyroscopes to tumble and fall over uselessly or for highly advanced electronic equipment to go dead as if some greater force soaks up all its energy— and then mysteriously regain its ability to function normally. Nothing in meteorological science explains how perfectly clear weather can be *instantly* replaced by thick yellow or dark murk that blots out all sight of the world, suddenly enveloping machines and pilots in a limbo frightening, dangerous, and beyond our understanding.

Not even the world of super-medicine, with the miracles of transplanting organs, restoring sight to the blind and hearing to the deaf, and enabling amputees to function as if they had never lost a limb, can explain how people seemingly beyond all hope of help from science or medicine suddenly "throw off" their ailments and are restored to perfect health. Understanding the mind better than we have ever done before has brought a new form of self-healing *that works.* People use biofeedback and other mind exercises to "reach within themselves" to successfully battle and overcome cancer and other deadly diseases. When medicine reaches its limits, the mysterious human mind is available to perform deeds that no doctors can match.

Can people truly journey "out of body"? Leave their physical body behind and float ethereally, with full control of their senses? This was once considered ridiculous, but there are too many cases where people on the brink of death have spiritually left their bodies and looked *down* to see themselves on an operating table—and later were able to describe everything that happened while they were unconscious during surgery.

The mysteries are endless. Plumbing the depths of what confounds us opens new and marvelous worlds. Being willing to try to understand what is natural, and what we still regard as supernatural—beyond the physical forces with which we are familiar—keeps wide and inviting the horizons of the future.

There is still magic around us, among us, within us all to share.

Natural or Supernatural?

1

"My Name Is Smith and I'm from Anywhere"

John M. Barclay stepped outside his farmhouse in the open country just beyond Rockland, Texas. His farm was in Tyler County and, typical of farmland holdings in eastern Texas, dependent upon the small town of Rockland. There were larger villages and towns, but they were far away. Shreveport lay just across the Louisiana border, and Nacogdochs and Lufkin, considered "big cities," each straddled the Angelina River. The countryside was a mixture of flatland or gently rolling hills; in the distance were the great forests around Sabine, Angelina, Davy Crockett, and Sam Houston. South toward Beaumont lay mostly empty country.

Even the farms were considered "open country" where a neighbor miles distant was "next door." Farming families accepted their solitude and separation. Texas was meant for the open spaces, and sometimes weeks might go by before neighbors even saw one another. Life was hard, simple, and for the most part uneventful.

April 21, 1897, passed like any other workday for Barclay. He was a typical Texas farmer, clad in bib overalls and roughshod boots made for the tough country. Barclay lifted his head at the sound of his dog outside. The animal was frenzied, barking and howling as it stared up at something in the sky. Barclay went outside to see what was agitating the animal. A dog in remote farm country was much more than a pet; it also served as sentry and alarm.

Before he reached his howling dog, Barclay already

heard what was keeping his dog in its furious uproar. From the sky came a strange whining noise disturbing to the ears. Barclay couldn't blame the dog for its uproar; the sound, growing steadily louder, seemed to pierce his own ears.

Barclay stood next to the animal and scanned the sky. He tensed at the incredible sight before him. Glowing brilliantly, casting an almost searing light, was something he had never seen before in his life—a great airship. That was the only description he could bring to mind. It was an oblong structure floating down from the sky, obviously under some kind of control.

He watched in amazement as the airship came closer and lower. He had seen trains and boats, and he was familiar with the wagons and buckboards of farm life. The airship was unlike anything he had ever seen before.

Then he shifted his attention from the surface structure of the airship. Of more immediate and commanding interest was the light. It had grown even brighter as the strange craft continued its descent. Now the airship entered into a wide circling movement about the astonished Barclay and his frantic dog. His amazement grew as the vessel settled slowly and under perfect control to the ground, remaining on a perfectly even keel so that the wings—at least what he believed to be wings—on each side remained clear of the ground as the main structure touched earth and stopped moving.

When all was still, Barclay started toward the machine. He knew only that whatever this incredible vessel was, it could fly and land under control. He was perhaps a hundred feet from the airship when a man appeared before him. Barclay didn't see how the man had reached his position between Barclay and the airship. It seemed that he "was just there."

Barclay's wonder became even greater when the man prevented him from getting any closer to the machine, which rested on the ground with its almost blinding light starkly illuminating the farm and the fields beyond. One surprise followed another as the stranger, apparently from the airship, spoke to Barclay—in perfect English.

"Smith is my name," he said, "and we'd like your assistance with some supplies." Astonished, Barclay nodded dumbly as "Smith" listed what he required: tools, chisels, lubricating oil—all items available at the Rockland hardware and general store. Would Barclay kindly get these for Smith?

Barclay agreed, and Smith handed him the money for the goods. American money. More than enough to purchase everything Smith had requested. Barclay took off quickly for Rockland, bought and paid for the goods, and rushed back to his farm, still not quite sure if what he had seen was real and would still be there.

Well before he reached his farm, he knew there was no fault with his memory. The dazzling light still bathed the countryside. The ship had not moved, and Smith waited right where Barclay had left him. Barclay handed over the equipment and supplies. By now he was calm enough to ask the questions burning in his mind.

"Where are you from?" he ventured.

Smith held him with a steady gaze. "From anywhere," he said finally. His tone made it clear there wouldn't be any further explanations. So Barclay tried another tack.

"Mind telling me where you're going?"

Smith nodded. "Certainly. The day after tomorrow we'll be in Greece."

Barclay was dumbfounded. To Greece? In only two days? Incredible! Impossible!

Smith reminded Barclay not to approach any closer to his vessel. He then turned, walked to the airship, and climbed aboard. Whatever he—and any others inside—needed to do, it was done quickly. The strange whining sound increased in volume, the dog became ever more frantic, and the airship began to rise slowly. As it cleared the ground it went into a smooth and astonishing acceleration. It kept going faster and faster and dwindled to a dot as it raced beyond the horizon. Barclay later described the acceleration and the speed as something that moved "like it was shot out of a gun."

Barclay wondered if anyone would ever believe him if and when he told them what he had experienced.

What he could not know was that either this airship or another like it already had been seen by witnesses just as incredulous as he was.

Two days before Barclay's encounter with the amazing airship, a strange light had attracted the attention of two people in Beaumont, Texas, well south of Rockland. Mr. J. B. Ligon and his son were at home when they were attracted by a powerful light emanating from a nearby pasture. The light seemed to come from a neighbor's farm several hundred yards distant. Ligon, well known in the Beaumont area, was the local sales representative for the Magnolia Brewery. Accompanied by his son, he hurried through the night toward the light.

They stopped abruptly when they were able to distinguish the outlines of four men. They stood in a group. Behind them loomed "a large, dark object." The light was so bright it prevented Ligon and his son from making out any details.

As Ligon and his son explained to a reporter from the *Houston Post* (which ran the interview and story on April 21, 1897, the same day that Barclay encountered an airship on his farm in Rockland), the strangers spoke perfect English. One of them moved forward: would Ligon mind bringing them a "bucket of water?" Ligon nodded, returned to his own farm, and brought back the water.

Responding to questions from Ligon, the man told him that his name was "Mr. Wilson," that they were journeying around the country "and beyond," and that they had just completed a trip over the Gulf of Mexico. Now they were about to return to their "quiet Iowa town" where, Wilson said, five airships like the one in which they were traveling had been built, and from where all five were making their memorable aerial journeys.

Ligon didn't hesitate a moment. How was the ship

powered? he asked. Wilson told him that the wings of the airship were powered by electricity. Ligon had no idea if this made any sense at all, but there was no doubting the existence of the airship and that it certainly could fly. Ligon and his son, equally stunned by the entire sight, watched the four men climb into a long compartment at the bottom of the airship's hull. They stared in awe as the airship began to move away into the night sky. It flew out of sight.

That was April 19. On April 20, a light appeared in Uvalde, another Texas farming town, and the man who went to investigate was Sheriff H. W. Baylor. He saw the light bathing his house and the surrounding grounds and then he heard voices. Immediately he left the house and went directly toward the light.

There was a great airship before him on the ground. He later told a reporter that he encountered three men who spoke with him in clear English. One man said his name was Wilson and that he hailed from Goshen, New York.

Then, to the astonishment of the sheriff, who had never seen an airship and knew of nothing like it flying about Texas skies, Wilson asked Sheriff Baylor if he knew a man named C. C. Akers, who had been the sheriff of Zavalia County. Wilson explained that he knew Akers from ten years before, in Fort Worth, and he looked forward to meeting him again.

Sheriff Baylor, taken aback by recognizing the name, confirmed that he certainly knew C. C. Akers, but that he'd left Fort Worth (to the north) and was now located at Eagle Pass. Wilson nodded, told Baylor he was disappointed to miss the meeting with Akers, and said he'd appreciate Baylor passing on his greeting to Akers when he next saw him.

According to Sheriff Baylor's report, "Wilson" then asked Baylor for water. He also requested that Baylor not talk about the presence of the airship with the local community. To Baylor, this seemed an outlandish request— because the airship was going to fly during the night with its glaring light and could hardly be kept a secret. Baylor watched the men climb into the gondola-like compartment beneath the airship. A whirring sound burst forth, "huge wings" began to flap up and down, "great fans" spun, and the airship "sped away northward in the direction of San Angelo."

Later, when reporters scoured the area for additional details they talked with the county clerk, who had seen the lighted airship rising into the sky and flying off to the north.

But the airships weren't quite through with their visits. On April 21 or 22 (the news reporters' dates sometimes overlapped with when the stories were filed and printed) another visitation occurred. Frank Nichols's farm was in the neighborhood of Josserand, Texas. Nichols was asleep when a powerful whirring sound disturbed the night and brought him fully awake in his bedroom. Immediately he went to the window and was astonished to see, as the *Houston Post* later reported, "brilliant lights streaming from a ponderous vessel of strange proportions" that had somehow landed in his cornfield.

Immediately Nichols threw on some clothes and rushed from his farmhouse to investigate. He was still running toward the "ponderous vessel" when two men appeared out of the dazzling light. Could they have some water from his well? they asked. Nichols agreed, and the men drew water and took it to the airship. He was delighted when one of the men asked him if he'd like a closer look at the huge machine. Nichols caught sight of at least eight "crew members" from the airship. One explained to him that the airship was powered with "highly condensed electricity."

He then added that this vessel was one of five that had been built secretly "in a small town in Iowa"; funds for the secret project had been supplied by a wealthy firm from New York State. Minutes later the "crew" climbed into the gondola and the airship rose in the same manner reported by witnesses to earlier flights.

What had at first seemed unbelievable gained more and more acceptance as the airships were encountered at close quarters. Many witnesses gave their stories to reporters. On April 23, the *Houston Post* carried yet another story: "two responsible men" had watched an airship with a "blinding light" fly down through the night sky to land in the Texas town of Kountze. They spoke with men from the airship, and two of the crew identified themselves as "Wilson" and "Jackson."

Four days later, April 27, stories appeared in the *Galveston Daily News*, including a letter from C. C. Akers! He had read the reports of "Wilson's" exchange with Sheriff Baylor, and he wrote to confirm that he indeed had known a man named Wilson in Fort Worth, Texas. The letter revealed that he recalled Wilson as a man with "a mechanical turn of mind who was then working on aerial navigation and something that would astonish the world."

The *Houston Post* printed follow-up airship reports, the major story being about a farmer from Deadwood, Texas. Farmer H. C. Lagrone had an experience similar to that reported by Barclay in Rockland. Lagrone told reporters that he was awakened at night by one of his horses going berserk, running wildly about its enclosure and bucking as if it were being hurt. The whirring sound that Lagrone heard seemed to be the cause of the animal's distress. It was aggravated by a glaring white light that was steadily circling nearby farmland. The familiar sequence of events was repeated. The airship landed slowly and under control, and once it was on the ground five men appeared before Lagrone. Two men walked to his well to fill rubber bags with water while three others talked easily with Lagrone. They told much the same story as they had to Frank Nichols. Five airships like the one before him had been built in great secrecy, this very machine a few days before had landed in the Beaumont area, and all five ships had been assembled in a little-known town in Illinois (not Iowa, as others had been told). A short time later the "whirring sound" increased and the airship activated its wings and fans and then sped off into the night.

Several days later the airships had completely vanished.

There is not the first shred of evidence that would establish that any airships were ever built in 1897 in Iowa or Illinois. Nor has any sense been made of the repeated requests for water from airships landing in the same general area of Texas. The explanation of a power source being "highly condensed electricity" makes no sense to electrical or mechanical engineers. The term has no reference to electrical systems for propulsion, then or now. And there have never been any known airships with electrically powered flapping wings and fans to move them with "great acceleration and high speed."

The powerful light that turned night into day is another mystery that has never found explanation. Nor has anyone ever come up with an explanation of what kind of power source could emit the "strange whirring sound" that could be heard for miles and that sent animals into a frenzy.

Which was why, despite the interviews and reports, with full names, locations, and witnesses including law officers and professional businesspeople, hardly anyone really believed the stories that were printed in the Texas newspapers. To most people the entire affair was ridiculous. Scientists questioned on the matter dismissed it as "impossible." Such airships could not and did not exist, period.

Then what had been flying around the United States since the previous year?

The startling airship encounters in April 1897 took place just about a half-century before the term *UFO* entered our daily language. At that time, there were no great UFO uproars, there wasn't any radar to track anything in the skies (radar wouldn't exist for many years to come), and there weren't any powered airplanes flying anywhere in the world.

There *were* airships—crude, underpowered, clumsy, slow, unwieldy, and of very limited endurance and range—

and most of these were in Europe. But the best of these couldn't come within a country mile of what the witnesses in Texas had encountered: *winged* airships capable of tremendous speed.

But airship sightings were not rare or freak occurrences. From mid-November 1896 to the late summer of 1897, reports of "impossible" airship encounters began to flower throughout the United States, and the number of witnesses grew swiftly to literally thousands. Most of the sightings took place at night: incredulous people pointed to dazzling lights moving through the sky, and engines—or whatever propelled these machines—were heard clearly.

The majority of the sightings in November 1896 came from California. Then the reports containing excited descriptions of the "great airships" spread to the northwestern United States, mainly Washington, followed by another wave of reports that filtered down from western Canada. The descriptions and sightings were certainly diverse and even more colorful than the visit to the Barclay farm in Texas. Hundreds of men and women in Tulare, California, near the end of 1896, went wild when they saw something, of indeterminate size but described as "obviously very large," plunge from the night skies flashing red, white, and blue lights. The airship was seen only from a distance, but *seemed* to land. Then, very abruptly, it "burst upward" and with steadily increasing speed raced off toward the Pacific Ocean. No one had any idea what it might have been.

THE AIRSHIPS THAT COULDN'T BE

By mid-February 1897, thousands of people were reporting airship sightings, with night appearances the most prevalent, as witnesses described brilliant lights in detail. A single airship floating thousands of feet above the ground—glowing from within and spraying out "gleaming light"—could be observed by people in a "sighting area" of a few thousand square miles.

Then the pattern changed dramatically.

Robert Hibbard in March 1897 *almost* became the first authenticated *abductee* by a flying vessel. One of the airships descended to a very low altitude over Hibbard's farm on the outskirts of Sioux City, Iowa. Hibbard stared in disbelief at the vessel; it was broad daylight. The airship drifted slowly closer to Hibbard. He saw that a cable of unknown material had been lowered from the ship, at the end of which was an anchor. Whoever or whatever was piloting that airship clearly had excellent directional control, because as Hibbard gawked, the anchor was snagged tightly into his clothes. Struggling to break free and frightened nearly out of his wits, Hibbard was then dragged along the ground like a man with his foot caught in a saddle stirrup. Abruptly the anchor was free of his clothing, but Hibbard was never certain whether he had succeeded in breaking free or he was deliberately released. He watched as the airship continued its flight, still staying at low altitude, heading toward a neighboring farm.

Later Hibbard learned just how fortunate he had been. Hibbard's terrified neighbor described in detail how the strange airship had floated over his land and used a trailing anchor to snag several head of cattle—which were hauled up into the airship! The following day, the farmer led disbelievers who had heard his amazing tale to a field where lay the remains of his missing cattle, slashed to bloody chunks and otherwise mutilated.

In April 1897 the number of witnesses and sightings soared. The citizens of Kansas City, Missouri, poured out of their homes to watch a huge, *black* airship hovering over their city. The witnesses—estimated by the press and local authorities to number some ten thousand—all saw the same sight. News reporters gave full details of a sight that couldn't be explained. In the *Chicago Record* of April 2, 1897, a correspondent wrote that the "object appeared very swiftly, then appeared to stop and hover over the city for ten minutes at a time, then after flashing green-blue and white lights, shot upwards into space."

An estimated one hundred thousand people in different states had seen not just one type of airship, but a bewildering variety of them that floated, drifted, descended, hovered, and accelerated at tremendous speed— all the while either glowing brilliantly from within or blocking out the sun with their "dark and sinister" shapes.

From Everest, Kansas, the news wires brought the latest sightings, this time giving eyewitness descriptions of an airship that looked astonishingly like a 25- to 30-foot-long Indian canoe! Light reflections and mirages were no secret to the world, and these were offered as explanations. Sunlight bouncing off a distant river or lake had projected the scene of a canoe against an inversion layer of mixed heated and cold air, acting as a mirror, sending across great distances a mirror image of the canoe, even expanding its size. All well and good, scorned the eyewitnesses, but that failed to explain the additional appearance "of a searchlight of varying colors."

The powerful lighting effects were as much a mystery as the airships. Almost all sightings during daylight made no mention of lights, but those that did described the lights as powerful and varying in colors and patterns. Almost all night sightings were rich with lighting effects, and almost every observer reported the airship(s) as "metallic."

While everything about the mystery airships confounded engineers and scientists, questions about the performance of the machines caused the most frustration and controversy. An *aerostat* is a vessel that derives its lifting power from the gas it contains in sealed containers, such as a series of round bags or, in the case of a balloon or blimp, one huge bag. This bag can be any shape. When greater speed and maneuverability are desired, a semirigid framework is used to give the airship a particular shape. And for highest performance, the *dirigible* design is used: a lightweight skeletal framework covers the entire vessel. (This was the design used for the great airships of the 1930s—the *Graf Zeppelin*, the *Akron* and the *Hindenburg*.)

Clearly the mystery airships at the end of the nineteenth century could have been blimps—inflated gas bags in the shape of cigars or tubes or sausages, over which securing lines were fitted to retain the shape and secure the passenger compartment (long gondola) along the bottom of the structure. The blimp airship design, aided by propellers, can float in the air, descend or climb slowly, and is able to overcome the force of wind (to a limited degree).

However, witnesses to the airship appearances of 1896-97 were consistent in their reports that "great wings" were attached to the airships and that the wings were flapped up and down by powerful electric motors. These also turned large fans (propellers) to thrust the airship forward and help in maneuvering.

At its very best such a system is clumsy and severely restricted in its speed capabilities. Flapping wings—utilizing the *ornithopter* design—may be great for birds, but for manned flying machines they're an engineering disaster. The structure is prone to failure and demanding of huge amounts of energy. It has such great resistance to movement through the air that its very form and shape restrict rather than enhance high speed.

These issues left knowledgeable engineers and scientists baffled by the eyewitness reports of mystery airships being able to accelerate rapidly and reach "tremendous speed." To an experienced observer, judgment of speed is always relative, and the eyewitnesses of 1896 and 1897 were hardly experienced at watching manned flying craft. Equally confusing were eyewitness statements that the airships climbed so swiftly they could be seen "racing upward into space." The best judgment is that these statements meant simply that the airships went so high they were hardly visible, and no one really meant that the airships flew above the atmosphere into vacuum.

There was general agreement that the mystery airships were *not* like the first crude airships (more shaped balloons than true airships) that began bumbling about the skies in England in the late eighteenth century. The *known* experimental airships were home-built affairs.

They carried their crews in flimsy and precarious "cat-walks with rails" suspended beneath the gas bags. The real airships were clumsy in shape and construction, had weak and cranky engines, were at the mercy of even a stiff breeze, and were prone to collapse while in flight. The confusion and controversy surrounding the different shapes, sizes, and characteristics of the mystery airships make it clear that these could not have been simple sightings of known experimental airships.

People began to regard the airship sightings as something beyond natural. No science or engineering available in the world could have produced these airborne wanderers. The sense of *alien* or *strange*, and suspicion of some sinister plot by a secret group bent on some mysterious goal, increased with the flood of reports. Sometimes sightings or encounters between airships and people on the ground took several days to reach the national press services, so that there might be a few days of empty skies and then a glut of sensational new reports.

What were these airships? Where had they come from? Who had built them? How could they perform as they did? The occupants spoke English, understood the questions asked them, and seemed perfectly cognizant of the everyday affairs of the Americans with whom they came in contact. But . . . who were they?

"They're not natural," was the general consensus.

Out of Topeka, Kansas, came the delayed report of another weird sighting on March 27. An object described as "large" came into view west of Topeka. More than two hundred people, including the governor of Kansas, held the vessel in clear sight. "I don't know what the thing is," the governor said with slick political aplomb, "but I hope it may yet solve the railroad problem!"

Ten days after one or more airships floated into view over Sacramento in early April, causing the usual fuss and surprise, another vessel made an appearance over east San Jose. This time a highly respected individual, among many other witnesses, provided new grist for the mill. Professor H. B. Worcester, president of the Garden City Business College, watched the airship from his home, along with a number of people in his presence. The good professor provided an excellent description for a reporter from the *San Francisco Call*:

"When the ship turned to the southeast," he offered, "I could distinguish two lights, one behind the other. The single first light seen was about the size of an engine headlight and had more the appearance of a large incandescent light than anything else." But that wasn't all, for Professor Worcester then added that he judged the speed of the lights as between sixty and one hundred miles per hour.

His next remarks raised the eyebrows of nearly all who read his report, for he added that he was almost certain that the motions he witnessed made it seem that the airship was *flapping its wings*. This was a possibility, he said, because of the manner in which the lights bathed the exterior of the ship. In any event, as the airship departed the area it was clearly in a descent.

Among several hundred other people staring at the sky were John Bawl and his family, pointing their fingers at the sky and exclaiming to one another in wonder at the sight. Bawl told reporters that the vessel seemed to be berserk and that it lurched and lunged from side to side. He added that it definitely had long, flapping wings and that a red light was suspended well beneath the airship he said was "bulky" and moving no faster than "an electric car doing its best."

Bawl's description of the red light sent reporters back to Topeka to ask more questions of the governor. The governor and the crowd of witnesses who'd watched with him all agreed that they had seen a "blood-red light," either very close to the airship or some distance beneath it. The governor added that his neighbor had lost several cattle to the same ship, which hauled up heavy animals with ease, chopped them up in crude fashion, and then dumped the mutilated carcasses haphazardly on his fields.

In March, one month after Robert Hibbard of Iowa had been hooked like a fish by the suspended anchor of an airship and barely escaped with his life, a frightening repetition was played out with Alexander Hamilton of Yates Center, Kansas. Hamilton and a group of his farmhands came out of a barn to see a huge airship hovering motionless, barely thirty feet directly above the lot in which he kept his cows. Hamilton was adamant that the cigar-shaped vessel was fully *three hundred feet long* and that there was no mistaking the very large "carriage" mounted beneath the hull.

Hamilton described the carriage as fashioned of great glass panels. Even more astonishing were the "strangest beings" he and the farmhands had ever seen. Unlike the encounter Barclay had had with "Smith" in Rockland, Texas, where "Smith" conversed in perfect English, these beings, who Hamilton claimed could be heard from the ground, spoke in a language none of the Kansas farmhands recognized or understood.

The airship began to ascend. It was just starting to climb away when Hamilton and the excited farmhands saw that a red cable extended from the glass carriage and had been dropped perfectly about the neck of a bawling heifer. Hamilton and his farmhands rushed forward in a desperate attempt to release the animal, but to no avail. The airship flew off northwest, the heifer dragging along the ground behind it. The ship soon outdistanced the angry men in the field.

The next day Hamilton and his hands stumbled onto the remains of the heifer. There wasn't much left—legs, hide, and head.

NONE SO BLIND

In April a huge airship also appeared over Chicago, Illinois. No one knows just how many people lifted their eyes to the night skies, but unquestionably this was *the* event of the evening. Reporters for the *Chicago Tribune* hammered out headlines: *Strange Vagrant of the Night*

Sky Sweeps Above the City . . . Seen All the Way from Evanston to South Chicago Where It Disappears in the West . . . Comes from the Lake . . . Sheds Bright Colored Lights . . . Some Observers Say They Discern Wings . . .

Several reporters rushed to question an eminent local scientist, Professor George W. Hough of the Dearborn Observatory at Northwestern University. The professor snorted at the idea that what had been seen was a machine that might be carrying men and operating under some kind of control. In a derisive remark that dismissed all the witnesses of all the sightings (to say nothing of the growing number of direct encounters), Professor Hough pointed his finger at the sky. "What you saw was a star. Yes, yes," he emphasized, "a very bright star in the constellation Orion."

This was to become the standard explanation for many years to come. If scientists were not inundated with proof they could carry back to their laboratories, then *whatever* was in the sky *had* to be a natural celestial object such as a star, a gleaming planet, or even a meteor streaking through the upper heavens.

Professor Hough notwithstanding, the airships persisted in their travels around the United States. Another landing was reported, this time on a farm near Waterloo, Iowa. As the farmer approached the airship, he sighted an "occupant." The "occupant" spoke perfect English and warned the farmer and others hastening to the scene that he had permission to land his machine on this farm, and that they were to keep their distance.

The "occupant" then produced a gun and threatened to shoot anyone who tried to enter the airship. Someone shouted a question. "Why are you here and what are you doing?"

"Why, we are flying around the world," came the matter-of-fact answer.

The rash of airship appearances across the United States was nearing its end, but it didn't just fade away. On May 6, 1897, another airship landed in an open field in Arkansas.

Two law officers were the first to spot the ship. Constable Sumpter and Deputy Sheriff McLenore, on horseback along a country road, caught sight of a brilliant light in the daytime sky. They watched it for several minutes. Then the light disappeared. It did not fade away; it went out as though a switch had been thrown. Perhaps an hour later the light reappeared, but this time much closer to the ground, and it was descending steadily. A shape became discernible and both men stopped their horses.

"It's going to land," one observed.

Land it did. They looked at the cigar-shaped airship resting on the ground, and spurred the horses to approach the vessel. The two lawmen judged they were about one hundred yards from the strange airship when the horses stopped. Nothing could bring the horses to move any closer to the vessel. Both men drew their rifles when they saw people emerge from the ship and gather between them and the ship.

One officer shouted: "Who is that? And what are they doing?"

One man with a long, black beard moved forward slightly. "Why," he answered, seemingly as puzzled by the questions as the lawmen were at the sight of the ship, "we're traveling across the United States."

The two officers looked at one another. One officer then asked why the light they had seen kept appearing and disappearing.

The answer was that nothing was disappearing: the light consumed much of the energy source of their airship, and they used it only when necessary. The lawmen agreed that strange as this vessel was, no laws were being broken. Having other work to do, the two men rode on. When they returned, approximately half an hour later, the airship was gone. They scanned the sky for any sign of the ship or that brilliant light. The sky was empty.

An even more bizarre encounter was reported in the April 16, 1897, issue of the *Saginaw Courier and Herald* in Michigan. A reporter wrote up what was called an "incredible encounter" between local farmers of Howard

City, Michigan, and a "strange airship" that landed in a farm area.

The vessel had landed at 4:30 A.M., according to the newspaper, and when farmers approached the strange craft, an "amazing" being stepped out from the ship.

According to the local farmers interviewed by the reporter, the "creature" stood nearly ten feet tall and was stark naked. One farmer moved closer to the "alien" in an attempt to talk with it. To his questions came a reply in a singsong musical voice that dumbfounded the farmer. He moved right up to the being, and the naked "alien" promptly lashed out with a wicked kick that sent the farmer tumbling and unable to rise—with his hip broken. Friends rushed in to drag him to safety.

The newspaper insisted that not only was this incident the absolute truth, but that the airship remained on the ground for several days, the naked alien emerging every day from the airship and drawing larger crowds as each day passed. Then one night the vessel lifted from the ground and soared out of sight.

That ended the story. The affair was met with disbelief and came to be regarded as a hoax. Where's the follow-up? people asked. Where are any pictures? What about interviewing the so-called crowds that gathered to look at the incredible scene and the musical alien?

The lack of any further reports led this incident to be labeled a hoax perpetrated either by the local farmer or by an enterprising jokester of a reporter who knew how to draw attention to his journal.

IMPOSSIBLE OR SUPERNATURAL?

Even by stretching the abilities of state-of-the-art airships, engines, and structural materials of the time to their maximum, there was absolutely no way that the airships described in these reports of 1896 and 1897 could possibly have been constructed as reported. Hydrogen or any other lighter-than-air gas could not have lifted the weight of airships that were described as some thirty feet in length, and even a vessel twice that size could not have lifted the weight of the glassed-in carriages, gondolas, and "people" observed aboard the various craft.

That was the immediate conclusion of engineers, mechanics, and scientists. The most advanced systems then available in the world simply were too primitive for the size and propulsion systems that were reported of the strange airships.

Then there was the matter of performance. The airships had been described by thousands of witnesses as moving with no more speed than that of an electric trolley at the low end, to speeds that sent the airships "hurtling" through the sky and climbing with the power one might attribute to a modern jet fighter—climbing steeply at high speed until the airship dwindled to a speck and then was lost to sight. To anyone who understood engines and propulsion systems the word was an immutable "impossible!"

Yet . . . there were so many reports and so many witnesses that the sightings could not be ignored.

Then there were the size variations, from a shape like a thirty-foot-long Indian canoe to an immense vessel at least three hundred feet in length. Such a ship would cover an entire football field, and its power sources would have to be great enough to maneuver the vessel in varying wind conditions and storms, as well as carry the crew, fuel, food and water supplies, and whatever else might have been aboard the "carriages" and "gondolas."

Topping it off were the "beings" aboard the vessels. Serious studies of the reports quickly threw out the naked giant ten feet tall and its musical language (if it was a language). But Barclay of Texas and others had spoken to the "people" from the airships in English, and they had responded in kind. At least one, perhaps more, of the airships' inhabitants spoke in a language no one could recognize. That left the matter hanging.

One man had almost been dragged into the air by an anchor that snagged his clothes. Several airships had used hooks and lassos to snatch cattle from open fields; the animals seem to have been slaughtered for their edible portions and the remains dumped unceremoniously to the ground.

Another mystery baffled investigators: in Rockland, Texas, when John Barclay had his exchange with the airship occupant who called himself "Smith," "Smith" expected the materials he had requested Barclay obtain for him from the hardware store in Rockland to be compatible with the equipment aboard the airship. He had also handed Barclay American money of the day.

The conclusions left great frustration in their wake. The airships could not have been built by any mechanical means of the time. Yet they were *there*. The beings aboard the airships were similar in appearance, clothing, and language. And those who did speak English made it evident that they were conducting what seemed to be perfectly normal flights around the world!

Attempts to understand all the many factors led to one of two possible conclusions. First, what was seen and encountered was impossible. But there were too many eyewitnesses for that conclusion to be accepted. So it *had* to be possible.

The theorists had a field day with the latter. Was it possible that there existed another Earth, in a space-time continuum right alongside our own? If this were so, could tears in the "fabric" of time and space permit these strange airships to slip through into *our* time and space and enter *our* universe?

Investigators related the airship sightings to research on strange and never-solved cases of people who had vanished before the eyes of family and friends, never to be seen again. These were incidents that no one could ever prove, because the "evidence" was gone forever. Not only individuals, but groups of people had simply walked out of existence.

It didn't seem probable, but it was possible.

Because the airships finally ended their appearances

over the United States, and that was as unlikely as anything else offered as an explanation. Where had they gone? What had happened to them?

Well, if somehow they slipped back through that distortion in space-time, they had returned to their own dimension and their own time.

But whatever the answer was, it was absolutely not natural to this world, to this space, and to this time.

2
WHERE DID THEY COME FROM AND WHERE DO THEY GO?

By the middle of the nineteenth century it had become apparent to researchers of unexplained sights in the skies that the sightings of mysterious airships, as eerie and fascinating as they might be, were really only late additions to an incredible history of wonders that had been flashing through the sky not merely for decades or even a century or two, but for thousands of years. Those who scoured ancient languages and texts and gathered what reports had been handed down were fully cognizant of the distortions that time and storytelling created. Far fewer people were living on the planet previously than today (there are more people alive now than in all previous generations combined), and social and national groups were spread out over the planet.

They believed in an assortment of gods and goddesses, spirits and visitors, demons and angels, and whatever unusual phenomena they experienced naturally became part of their folklore. People *knew* it was impossible for human beings to fly, so whatever was seen flying through the skies must be either heavenly messengers or demons descending to carry out evil designs. Even in the Roman Empire, ruling all the known world at the height of its power, one needed a program just to tell who was whom among the many gods whose pleasure or wrath one might invoke.

Even further back in human history, primitive humans clad in furry garments of beasts gathered around fires and hid in caves, seeing spirits and demons and gods around tree stumps and bushes. The rain was the favor of the gods; lightning was their anger; animals became pregnant when favorable winds blew from the right direction.

The ancient cave dwellers left paintings upon the walls of caves that are magnificent and incredibly accurate, in color and proportion, of the animals they hunted. If these primitive artists were so capable of realism in their burgeoning human drive to capture the spirit and reality of the beasts of their time, then it is not so farfetched to judge that if they saw strange objects in the heavens, they would be as capable of recording accurately what they saw.

Careful dating methods took scientists to an era some 47,000 years ago when they discovered images made by the people who inhabited caves so long ago. (A cautious note: most cave paintings have been lost due to earthquakes, volcanoes, and the ravages of time or have simply never been found. So any record from so early in human history is a precious find indeed.) Scientists discovered cave paintings made not by modern Homo sapiens but by Neanderthals. The find was dug laboriously with sharpened rocks out of the side of a mountain on an island in China's Hunan Province.

Scientists were stunned with the find; the pictures carved with such energy and determination by these long-dead artists were clearly of cylindrical vessels soaring through the sky and bearing an uncanny resemblance to what an artist of today might produce of a craft able to travel through space beyond our atmosphere.

Researchers know only too well that anything extracted from historical record of any kind, in any form, and from anywhere in the world is probably no more than the minutest fraction of virtual hordes of unidentified things *floating, drifting, ascending, descending, twisting, looping,* and *racing* through the skies. (These words have all been used throughout history to describe the motions of objects in the sky.)

From ancient times to mere hundreds of years ago, education was a rare gift, available only to a select few and often laced with superstition and forced into theological contexts. How were sightings and unusual events to be recorded? When something clearly built and occupied by intelligent beings was seen racing through the skies, it was attributed not to an intelligent race but to the gods or spirits. Most of what *was* seen was forced to fit a religious context, explained as a spiritual happening or as an encounter with "gods." It's not necessary to go *that* far back in history to confirm that this is true: the appearance of Spaniards clad in armor and riding horses was proof positive to the South American and Mexican Indians that the long-prophesied gods had finally arrived.

Probably thousands of sightings and encounters have vanished into the maw of the unknowable past, but what has survived has made it clear that the ancients had their share of "miracles and wonders to behold."

The cave paintings and rock carvings lie far before times when people began to record in remarkable detail these "miracles and wonders." In extraordinary historical documents from China there are uncounted descriptions of inexplicable events in the heavens. Chih-Chiang Tsu-Yu, royal engineer for the powerful Emperor Yao of China, was a man of great imagination and no small acquaintance with real engineering possibilities. What Chih-Chiang Tsu-Yu recorded is possibly an actual encounter with a spacecraft, about which the Chinese royal engineer recorded incredible details.

Four thousand three hundred years ago Chih-Chiang Tsu-Yu described an astonishing flight from the Earth to the moon on a "celestial bird." Before the reader dismisses the rest of this encounter as an ancient fairy tale, note that if this same engineer were describing the Apollo spacecraft that carried U.S. astronauts to the moon, in the language of his time, it would still be a "celestial bird." His poetic manner of speech doesn't mean that he soared aloft on some huge feathered creature.

The more one learns of this celestial bird, the more amazing becomes this adventure and the more fascinating become certain details of which Chih-Chiang was aware. We know of no way he could have accurately described sights and conditions beyond the Earth. His celestial bird, as the detailed records show, enabled Chih-Chiang to raise himself high above the Earth by "mounting the current of luminous air." "Luminous air" describes perfectly the barely visible exhaust of the *Titan II* booster used to propel Gemini spacecraft into Earth orbit, and it is just as accurate to describe the upper stages of rocket boosters that burn a combination of liquid oxygen and liquid hydrogen.

Chih-Chiang also recorded that his "celestial bird" provided him with exact information about celestial events, particularly concerning the sun, so that he might set his flights at the most effective times.

Chih-Chiang's story became even more astonishing. After his return from the moon, he stated that while in space it wasn't possible to perceive the diurnal movement of the sun. How he knew over four thousand years ago that the sun rotated on its axis is a question no one has ever answered.

He described being on the lunar surface, where he surveyed the "frozen-looking horizon." Then Chih-Chiang took a sudden imaginative turn and told his readers that while on the moon he built a "Palace of Great Cold." Specialists in the Chinese language of that ancient time caution that the statement should not be taken as more than a "verbal picture of lunar conditions" of startling accuracy.

If it is true that this royal engineer was the first to voyage from the Earth, as Chinese legend tells us, then to his wife, Chang Ngo, go the honors of being the first woman to reach the moon. Chang Ngo's story, found in the preserved records of China, describes the moon as a "luminous sphere, shining like glass, of enormous size and very cold; the light of the moon has its birth in the sun."

If we take Chih-Chiang's and Chang Ngo's descriptions of lunar conditions and compare them with the reports of Apollo astronauts it is nearly impossible to tell the difference. Other details about space voyages in the ancient Chinese scrolls paint clear word-pictures of a huge vessel that did not sail like a ship at sea, but appeared on the ocean at night, shining with powerful, dazzling lights. The "ship that could sail to the moon and the stars" clearly referred to a spacecraft. It was also described as being able to "hang among the stars" and as "the boat to the moon."

As a finale to these oddly disturbing and astonishingly accurate records, it was noted in the histories that the "boat to the moon" stayed for *twelve years*. And then it was gone.

Throughout recorded history there have been references in many different lands and societies about visitations from somewhere else. The *Surya Sutradhara* is an ancient astronomical text from India that describes *siddhas* and *vidyaharas*—learned men and scientists—who could *orbit* the planet "below the moon but above the clouds." The *Samaranagana Sutradhara* also contains clear references to "visitations," describes flights in great skyships, and mentions heavenly beings who descended from the sky. (This book lacks the detailed descriptions of the Chinese texts, and historians are loathe to accept such writings from India as anything except poetic and religious.)

On the walls of caves in the Santander province of Spain have been painted, not airships such as those described earlier, but *discs*—dozens of them, rendered with surprising skill and artistry, spanning many caves. Discs were also discovered in cave paintings along the Tassil plain in the Sahara. Archaeologists find unquestionable paintings of still more discs in many locations, and one group of paintings in particular at Niaux, Spain, caused excitement upon their discovery.

The disc was painted with excruciating care, showing it in flight low above the ground. One painting clearly showed a disc standing on landing gear on the ground, with antennae extending upward from the craft.

THE GREAT WAVE BEGINS

Prior to approximately 1500 B.C., reports of flying objects were embedded within paintings, religious ceremonies, and poetry and tales handed down from participants. Then came the "great change," as the number of historical documents by scribes, who recorded events, kingly proclamations, and proceedings, increased dramatically.

This new wave of recorded, written history commenced in the court of Thutmose III of Egypt, who reigned from 1504 to 1450 B.C. The historian Prince de Rachelwitz, who translated the papyrus records of the eighteenth dynasty, shares this beguiling moment from long ago:

> In the year 22, third month of winter, sixth hour of the day . . . it was found a circle of fire was coming from the sky. . . . it had [a] foul odor. . . . now after some days had passed these things became more numerous in the sky than ever. They shone more in the sky than the brightness of the sun and extended to the limits of the four supports of the heavens. . . . powerful was the position of the fire circles. The army of the Pharaoh looked on with him in their midst. . . . after supper, these fire circles ascended higher in the sky to the south. . . ."

More than two thousand years ago Roman scribes began recording a growing number of "strange sightings in the skies." In 216 B.C. witnesses reported the astonishing sight of ships "seen in the sky over Italy. . . ."

East of Rome, in Apulia, at Arpi, "a *round shield* was seen in the sky. . . ."

"At Capua, the sky was all on fire, and one saw figures like ships. . . ."

Seventeen years later, ". . . in Tarquinia, there fell in different places . . . a thing like a flaming torch, and it came suddenly from the sky. Towards sunset, a round object like a globe or round or circular shield took its path in the sky, from west to east."

In 90 B.C., in Umbria, north of Rome, hundreds of people looked up in mixed awe and terror as a globe of golden fire swooped down to the earth, its flaming coloration grew stronger, and then it shot upward from the surface, so bright that it eclipsed even the sun in its brilliance.

During A.D. 393 there were many sightings of globes soaring through night skies. Despite excited reports that these may have been manufactured vessels, many scientists believe that what observers saw were blazing meteor showers, or comets breaking up in the atmosphere, producing "brilliant globes of light." These may still be seen today.

Startled observers watched a brilliant light racing through the night sky. Moments later other lights appeared and moved swiftly toward the original light. Soon the sky was ablaze with lights swarming about the first bright globe that had been seen. Then all the lights appeared to merge into a single dazzling globe that *shot upward*, dwindling in size with increasing distance from the observers.

In A.D. 1034 over Europe was seen a sphere, blazing with flames, that raced across the skies in a straight line through the air. The sphere became clearer as it approached the viewers, and as it grew clearer, its shape altered until all the observers agreed they were watching a cigar shape, still surrounded by flames only slightly less brilliant than before, which disappeared over the horizon.

In 1180 the Japanese were also seeing a strange sight in the heavens, which historians recorded on October 27 as an "earthenware vessel" that shone brilliantly in the sky. It flashed into view from the direction of Kii province, then suddenly changed direction, issued forth a "shining trail in the heavens," and raced away until it was gone beyond the horizon.

In England in the late twelfth century, over Begeland Abbey a huge disc, strangely flat and gleaming silver, flew over the abbey and left behind a crowd of terrified monks.

The year 1211 brought another variation, this time in Cloera, Ireland. An airship (strikingly similar to those reported in the 1896-97 sightings in the United States) sailed low over the ground, trailing a line with an anchor at its end. Dozens of frightened witnesses watched as the trailing anchor snagged on a church eave and hauled the airship to a stop. An angry occupant, male, climbed down the rope with knife in hand and cut the rope, freeing the airship but leaving the anchor behind. The witnesses, gathering their wits about them, started up the church stairs to capture the airship crewman but were stopped in their tracks by the local bishop, who shouted to them to let him go. The airship and the man clambering back up the rope disappeared in the distance, and the local records showed that the anchor was brought into the church and placed on display. (A case of great similarity took place in Merkel, Texas, in 1897. There the trailing anchor from an airship caught in a rail of a building. An occupant slipped down the rope and cut loose the airship, and the vessel rose as it departed. The anchor was proudly put on exhibit in the Merkel blacksmith shop.)

On September 24, 1235, a powerful Japanese military officer, General Yoritsume, was in an open field encampment with a strong military force. He heard shouts and cries. Instantly alert, Yoritsume ordered weapons to the ready, but there was no assailant nearby. Soldiers pointed to the night sky. Yoritsume was astonished to see brilliant lights whirling through the darkened heavens.

The lights moved in an area southwest of the encampment, dazzling, racing in circles, performing loops and incredible gyrations in a show that lasted for hours. By early morning the lights still spun and swirled, their brilliance only slightly diminished by the dawn. Then they were gone. Angry and frustrated, Yoritsume ordered his staff to bring to him a scientific explanation of what he and his men had seen through most of the night.

Whoever the chief "scientist" was, clearly he felt that "Who knows?" was the last thing to say to the general—he *had* to have an answer. He told Yoritsume that "the whole thing is completely natural. It is only the wind making the stars sway."

History spares us the reaction of the general.

Dr. Jacques Vallee, astronomer, computer scientist, and tireless UFO researcher, has noted an incredible relationship with the "phantom chariots" that so awed the ancient world. When Charlemagne ruled France, Vallee found in historical documents, his reign was plagued by encounters and possibly clashes with these "tyrants of the air and their aerial ships."

The encounters became so numerous and upset the French leader so severely that he issued an edict, about the strongest in the long history of encounters with strange aircraft, that if someone so much as even *reported* a sighting of a vessel not from France, he or she would be seized by soldiers, tortured, and, after being broken and savaged, put to death.

So the flow of reports during a time of extensive "alien airship" excursions slowed to a trickle, and many written records were destroyed.

One incident that survived in the records is not only revealing of the times but quite extraordinary in its chain of events.

One day it chanced at Lyons that three men and a woman were seen descending from these aerial ships. The entire city gathered about them, crying out they were magicians sent by Charlemagne's enemy to destroy the French harvest.

In vain, the four innocents sought to vindicate themselves, saying they were their own country folk and had been carried away a short time since by miraculous men who had shown them unheard-of marvels. Luckily, the Bishop of Lyons pronounced the incident as false, saying it was not true these men had fallen from the sky, and what [the town folks] said they had seen there was impossible. The people believed what their good Bishop said rather than their own eyes and set at liberty the four ambassadors . . . from the ship.

During this historical period in Europe the Roman Catholic Church became a formidable political force by wielding great influence through threats of damnation. The Church became virtually the sole arbiter of what was acceptable and what was heresy. Anything church leaders could not understand or control directly—whatever might threaten the new political power of the church-state—was immediately labeled as dangerous, satanic, ungodly.

In the records of the United States, the first clearly defined disc shape was recorded in 1878 when a Texas farmer reported to local authorities that he had watched a dark object sailing through the skies; it was, he said, shaped like a "large saucer."

August 3, A.D. 989: During a period of political turbulence in Japan, there appeared in the skies three "round objects" of eye-watering brilliance. They flew in full view of thousands of people, then seemed to join together into a single vessel that finally traveled out of sight.

September 12, 1271: The ruling authorities of a Japanese prefecture decided that a famous priest, Nichiren, had offended them so greatly that he was condemned to have his head severed with a traditional battle sword. The beheading was arranged to take place at Tatsunokuchi in Kakamura. As the execution was about to be carried out there suddenly appeared in the sky a great round object, described as shaped like the full moon but shining with a dazzling light. The officials conducting the execution shouted in fear and ran from the death stand as if devils were pursuing them. The assembled crowd followed suit in a wild panic. Nichiren was the first person known whose life was saved by an alien spacecraft!

November 4, 1322: In the skies to the south of Uxbridge, England, a pillar of blazing fire rose above the horizon and then, with a slow and grave motion, flew northward across the sky. Flame showered outward from the front of the burning pillar and then changed to dazzling beams of light. The pillar flew slowly and steadily until it disappeared over the northern horizon.

1361: People living along the western coast of the Inland Sea looked up in fear as an "object, shaped like a drum and about twenty feet in diameter," shot out of the deep waters and boomed into the air, climbing out of sight.

November-December 1387: In Northamptonshire and throughout the county of Leicester, England, strange fires appeared suddenly in the skies. They were in the shape of great wheels that revolved, blazing furiously as they traveled, huge round barrels of flame, hurling fire about them, or long, fiery beams speeding through the winter skies.

January 2, 1458: A bright, shining object the apparent size of a full moon appeared in the sky over Japan in broad daylight.

March 17, 1458: Five brilliant "stars" appeared suddenly in the sky, but these stars were in a loose group and traveling with stupendous speed. They circled the moon, then changed colors three times, then suddenly vanished as if a light had been shut off. So many people saw these "stars" across Japan that officials were warned that a terrible disturbance must be expected in the land (in a country of earthquakes and volcanic activity, when a "disturbance" was predicted, people feared the worst). In the great city of Kyoto, priests announced that a great calamity was in the making—and even the emperor was convinced disaster was forthcoming.

November 1, 1461: Europe came under visitation again when a blazing object likened to an iron rod of "good length and as large as one half of the moon" flashed into view over Arras, France. It stayed within view for perhaps twelve minutes. Many witnesses described the object quite specifically as "like a ship, from which fire was seen flowing."

January 3, 1569: A "flaming star" shot across Japan, which many people took to portend the collapse of the Chu Dynasty. For years afterward, blazing objects of varying size and brilliant colors raced through the skies. (Such reports should be taken with a great dose of salt. If a meteor approaches the earth so that it skims through the upper atmosphere, it will look precisely like a ship powered with a long flame; the colors come from the incineration of different minerals of the stony or metallic meteors. Exploding meteors, or *bolides*, show tremendous displays of exploding green, yellow, orange, red, and other colors and can briefly turn night as bright as day.)

May 1606: A blazing fireball, this time taking the shape of a burnished wheel, *hovered* above Nijo Castle in Kyoto. Reports of samurai confirmed the sightings of other witnesses.

Airships seemed to be reduced in numbers for long periods of time, but the skies remained busy with other incredible shapes. The long and short of it was that the shapes reported by witnesses, most of whom trembled with fear and apprehension that they were being given signs of horrifying catastrophes to follow, not only boggle the imagination, but stretch probability beyond the breaking point.

By the eighteenth century sightings began to be reported with far greater detail than earlier witnesses had ever provided. The new world was filled with industrial, scientific, and mechanical marvels, and modern skepticism required that sightings be described in meticulous detail to be given even the slightest consideration.

December 8, 1733: In Dorset, England, a Mr. Cracker reported having watched "something" in the sky on a clear day, of an "amazing coruscation" that flew with tremendous speed. It had the color of "new washed silver" and trailed an enormous plume of flame as it raced from east to the north. Several witnesses came forward to corroborate the sighting.

December 16, 1742: This time the witness was a

highly trained researcher and scientist and a Fellow of the Royal Society of London, England. He refused to reveal his name, understandably saying he would be the butt of endless laughter from his associates. "At first I thought it was a rocket, of large size." But instead of climbing, the object, some twenty degrees above the horizon, raced along parallel to the Earth's surface and slowly cruised across the sky with an undulating motion. The witness said, "From one end, it emitted a bright glare and fire. . . . That end was a frame like bars of iron, and quite opaque to my sight. . . ."

Sightings that included such detail brought researchers to return to other, older reports gathered in their files that had been discounted as mass hysteria, hoaxes, or just plain nonsense. But as the more distinguished and scientifically trained observers came to the fore, older cases assumed new significance.

April 14, 1561: Early on a quiet morning in Nuremberg, a swarm of weird objects seemed to come "from everywhere," and within minutes huge cylindrical objects poured into the space above the city. The gleaming thick cylinders moved constantly and released or expelled an even greater number of black, red, and orange globes. Some cylinders hurled forth smoking spheres that mixed with the globes and cylinders, and then the entire swirling mass was joined by spinning discs that weaved in and out with the other objects. By noon, it was reported, the objects had either flown away or simply vanished from sight. No one could offer any explanations. These were obviously not terrestrial in nature. Where had they come from? How were they controlled? What was their purpose? Why were they over Nuremberg?

August 7, 1577: In Basel, Switzerland, sixteen years later, a similar sighting occurred. But this time most of the objects in the sky were the smoking spheres, which were watched by thousands of people. What seemed to be a vicious battle among the smoking spheres began as they darted at one another, crashing violently against one another and filling the skies with smoke. Then, suddenly, they were gone.

With the advent of telescopes a whole new category of sightings was created. Astronomers saw spheres racing across the face of the moon. Dozens of scientists reported spheres, discs, and spindles crossing the face of the sun. These were not isolated incidents but repeated sightings recorded by scientists of different countries. One of the most important sequences was reported by de Rostan, an astronomer and member of the medico-physical society of Basel, Switzerland. On August 9, 1792, he observed through his telescope an object shaped like a spindle moving across the face of the sun, then returning, going back and forth repeatedly. He kept detailed reports as he watched this same action almost every day for a full month, and even drew its outline and sent it to the Royal Academy of Sciences in Paris.

Other astronomers searched for these strange objects, which appeared to be in deep space. At least one, who communicated with de Rostan, also saw objects, but of a slightly different shape than those observed by de Rostan. A third astronomer failed to detect anything unusual. To the scientists this strongly indicated that sunspots were not the cause of the sightings.

If the "across the face of the sun" sightings seemed improbable, "across the face of the moon" sightings were even more puzzling. On September 7, 1820, during an eclipse of the moon, trained observers were startled to see—and they confirmed each others' sightings—linear formations of unidentified objects moving steadily in front of the moon and then, turning, maintaining a military precision of formation. This was a "most disturbing mystery."

Mexico had its own share of heavenly sightings, including hundreds of objects flashing across the faces of both the sun and the moon. The most striking reports came from Oaxaca, when on July 6, 1874, an object nearly five hundred feet in length was seen "swaying" in the sky. The object, which observers said was in the form of a "giant trumpet," remained in view for several minutes.

In August 1883, over Zacatecas, Mexico, hundreds of incredulous observers gaped at the skies as more than four hundred "vehicles," many of them of torpedo or cigar shape, flew high overhead as if on their way to some specific destination.

August 20, 1880: M. A. Trecul, a member of the Royal Academy of Sciences, sent a report to the Academy that on this date he had sighted, clearly and beyond question, a gleaming, flashing, golden, cigar-shaped vessel in the sky, which, as it passed overhead, appeared to release a smaller vessel that shot ahead of the "mother craft."

By the beginning of the twentieth century, people all over the world were seeing objects they could describe but could not identify as to origin, manufacture, size, or purpose. In 1926 a group of explorers in northern China, in the Kukunor district, a short distance from the Humboldt Chain, marked carefully in their diaries that at 9:30 on the morning of August 5, the entire group caught sight of a "huge oval" in the sky reflecting the sun. There was enough time as the oval flew overhead for them to grab their binoculars and take a leisurely look at the strange machine, which clearly reflected sunlight from its metallic surface.

On June 10, 1931, Sir Francis Chicester, a world-famed flier, was flying his Gypsy Moth aircraft across the Tasman Sea from New Zealand to Australia. He had been in the air several hours, fought his way through heavy storms, and finally emerged into excellent flying conditions—a bright blue sky with only a few small clouds in sight.

But something else also came into sight. Chicester stared in surprise as he saw an airship headed his way from ahead and to his left, a gray and white vessel with a dull finish on its surface. From his viewing angle it had the shape of an oblong pearl. Then it simply faded from view.

Chicester then saw flashes of light that seemed to be reflecting off an aerial object, but he could not make out any
airship form again. He banked the airplane successively,
turning to bring the entire sky within his range of vision.
He saw the airship, either the same one or another very
much like it, emerging from a small group of clouds. He
glued his eyes to the airship, closing the range between his
own plane and the airship, and judged its distance as a
mile from him when it vanished. Soon it reappeared, again
at a distance of one mile. He closed the distance until it
was "quite close," and watched in amazement as the airship began to fade before his eyes.

Then it was gone.

Chicester had never heard the words *flying saucers*
or *UFO*. The episode was to him "uncanny," and he let it go
at that.

As the eighteenth and then the nineteenth century
passed, the gathering of reports brought new revelations
about old happenings. It turned out that the number of
weird, improbable, impossible, fanciful objects that raced,
lofted, glowed, drifted, burned, accelerated, twisted,
looped, turned, and did all manner of strange things in the
skies had been far larger than anyone ever believed. More
and more it seemed that supernatural forces of some
manner were at work. There was no other way people,
from everyday workers to the most brilliant scientists,
could explain ships that were "impossible" and yet carried
people and other bizarre "occupants" to and from an invisible wall in the sky that seemed to swallow anything that
slid through its yielding fabric. The twentieth century,
with its nuclear energy, computers, and space flight, her-
alded a new age of technological wonder, but it still
couldn't explain these "supernatural" reports.

The oceans of our world have been the sites of visitations as bizarre as those on land. The most common "sea
sightings" have been glowing wheels, from small size to
enormous craft, glowing brightly or burning, sometimes

one wheel, other times two wheels with a structure in between.

May 15, 1879: The crew of the steamship *Vulture* was alerted by the frenzied shouts of a lookout as the vessel sailed through the waters of the Persian Gulf. The men rushed to one side of the *Vulture* and stared in disbelief as two "giant luminous wheels," judged to be at least 120 to 150 feet in diameter and spinning rapidly, drifted low above the Gulf waters. The men watched in disbelief as the huge double-wheeled craft descended to the surface and then slipped *beneath* the water and disappeared from sight. There was no doubt among the observers that the strange craft was under full control.

May 1880: One year later, the British Steamship Company's steamship *Patna* was sailing through the same area of the Persian Gulf as had the *Vulture*. It was nearly midnight when Lee Force Brace called out that he had in sight the "most extraordinary" craft—two wheels, luminous, one on either side of the *Patna*. The commander of the steamship, Captain Avern, and Third Officer Manning, alerted by the shouts from Brace, also saw the wheels. Each wheel was estimated to be at least 1,500 to 2,000 feet in diameter. They were spinning steadily, and the men distinctly heard a loud swishing sound from the spinning. They all confirmed that the spokes of the wheels were actually touching part of the steamship. The report indicates, but does not specify, that the wheels also descended into the water. However, Brace's report stated emphatically that after the sighting, the Gulf waters became "phosphorescent." The wheels were under observation for at least twenty minutes.

April 10, 1901: Again in the Persian Gulf, at 8:30 A.M., crew members of SS *Kilwa* reported a "huge" rotating wheel in the sky, low to the water. Five years later, in the Gulf of Oman, another British steamship crew encountered a "giant wheel" above the Gulf waters. Then, in 1909, sailing in the China Sea, the captain of a Danish steamship was stunned to sight one of these wheels. The captain, whose veracity was considered "unassailable," wrote that the great wheel was rotating on the surface, and then just beneath the surface of the sea. The wheel was well illuminated and a center hub was clearly visible.

These few reports represent hundreds of sightings, most of which are attended by mystical mutterings by frightened sailors. But there have been enough documented sightings of the so-called oceanic UFOs to leave no doubt that they appear, they either fly or levitate, they are luminous, they can reach enormous sizes, and they rotate both above and below the surface of the ocean. The wheels, and other shapes as well, have been observed to plunge at steep angles into the ocean and disappear from sight. And on other occasions they have erupted with almost violent force from beneath the ocean, blazing upward with tremendous acceleration.

And nobody knows what they are.

3

THE GREAT UFO CIRCUS

There seems to be general agreement that the Great Flying Saucer Age was triggered on June 24, 1947, when shortly after noon, Kenneth Arnold, a private pilot, was launched from the relatively obscure Chehalis Airport in the state of Washington. Arnold had arrived at the airport to join in the search for a Curtiss C-46 Commando military transport missing "somewhere in the Cascade mountains" and presumed to have crashed. A number of pilots were flying that day in attempts to find the lost C-46 and, they hoped, the survivors of the crash. Arnold was flying his own plane, a single-engine low-wing ship. The weather for the search mission was perfect, what pilots call "severe clear," meaning that visibility is nearly unlimited.

A few minutes before three o'clock that afternoon (as noted on his instrument panel clock), Arnold was cruising near towering Mount Rainier. He was swinging into a wide, easy turn in his search pattern when he was startled by a brilliant blaze of blue-white light from the side. His first thought was that it was an explosion, but when he failed to see flame or smoke either in the air or on the ground he dismissed that thought. There had been no shock wave or sound of an explosion, which could be louder than the roar of his own engine.

He made a careful scan of the sky and saw another airplane. He recognized, well to the left and aft of his own airplane, a four-engined Douglas DC-4 passenger airliner on its regular trip between Seattle and San Francisco.

Arnold resumed his search. Again his eyes were struck by that dazzling flash.

This time, his senses alert, he saw that the flash had come from north of his own plane, and that something in the sky was heading south from Mount Baker—heading directly toward him.

What Kenneth Arnold then saw, clearly and for enough time to pick out details, forever changed history. He stared with disbelief as nine strange shapes hurtled closer and closer. He had never seen anything like the sight before him. He thought perhaps he was seeing secret new military aircraft.

They were each approximately fifty feet in diameter. The fact that they were flying in echelon formation led him to his first belief that they were military aircraft. Then he realized that that was impossible, because these ships lacked wings and were in the shape of huge crescents. They did not maintain smooth flight (not unusual in the turbulence near mountains). The silvery, flat, gleaming crescents were skimming the high peaks of the mountains and rocking and banking slightly as they sped over the mountains.

The familiar rocking and banking motion was *all* that made sense to Arnold. He had never seen or heard of these huge shapes flat as a hubcap and reflecting sunlight with a dazzling glare.

The crescents raced by Mount Rainier and then Mount Adams. Arnold calculated the elapsed time between the first and last vessels to be one minute and forty-two seconds. When he measured the distance on his flight chart between the two mountains, he could hardly believe what his own figures told him. The great silvery crescents were flying at a speed of 1,656 miles per hour! That was incredible, seemingly impossible, but Arnold had held the formation in sight for several minutes, the visibility was perfect, and he felt no doubt that his direct observations, chart measurements, and the times involved were accurate.

Arnold watched the crescents disappear into the distance. Excited by what he'd experienced, he headed directly for the airport at Yakima, landed, and lost no time in getting to the office of Al Baxter, a friend who ran an airfield operation called Central Aircraft. Arnold told Baxter the entire story. Baxter in turn called in other pilots to hear Arnold repeat his amazing tale. Soon afterward, watching the time slipping by, Arnold returned to his own plane, fired up, and took off for the airport at Pendleton, Oregon.

This time he had a small crowd waiting for him. One or more of the pilots who'd heard Arnold's report in Baxter's office had called ahead to other pilots, who in turn called local news reporters. Arnold again related what had happened to him, but this time he met retorts of disbelief when he described the gleaming crescents. Arnold withstood the barrage of questions easily. He had more than four thousand hours logged in flight, he was a seasoned search-and-rescue pilot with extensive mountain flying experience, and it was clear to the reporters that Arnold not only didn't *try* to gain their belief, he didn't seem to care *what* they believed.

It was undoubtedly his extensive piloting experience and excellent reputation that kept the press from branding him as a wacko who saw things that were impossible. Doing their best to prove that Arnold had made an "honest mistake," scientists and military teams attacked the press's reports of Arnold's experience, stressing that Arnold could not have made out details on anything that had a span of approximately fifty feet from twenty miles away. A scientist offered the explanation that Arnold had seen military jet fighters in formation, reflecting the sun so brilliantly they partially blinded Arnold; he had misjudged their distance from his own plane and they only *seemed* to be flying as fast as his chart measurements indicated.

No sooner had this brilliant observation been offered than another "expert" stepped forward to dismiss his predecessor with "he doesn't know what he's talking about. This fellow Arnold must have seen bombers. *Big* bombers, so that they only *seemed* to be flying that fast. And their shape? Why, the bright reflections, and Arnold looking through the glass of his own airplane, could make them out into almost any shape."

Well, if they *were* fighters or bombers, it would be easy enough to find out by asking the Air Force. But military officials refused to comment on any formations that may or may not have been in the air near Mount Rainier at that time. However, they jumped into the "real explanations" with undisguised zeal. Arnold had been the victim of a mirage created by an inversion layer of air mirrored over the mountain peaks. What he thought were crescent-shaped ships flying "like a saucer would if you skipped it across the water," as Arnold had explained to reporters, were actually mountain peaks that *seemed* to be separated from the mountains below and therefore *seemed* to be saucers racing through the skies.

That Kenneth Arnold had never actually said they were flying saucers was lost in the uproar in the press and throughout the aviation world immediately after. On the same day of Arnold's sighting, other reports began to filter in from pilots across the country who reported strange unidentified shapes in the skies. The capper came with a sighting ten days later. A United Airlines airliner lifted off from the commercial field at Boise, Idaho. Captain E. J. Smith and his first officer (copilot), Ralph Stevens, were still in their initial climbout, keeping a sharp lookout for any other aircraft that might be intersecting with their own flight path, when a formation of five objects appeared in their sight. Both men were startled to see that they were not airplanes but crescent-shaped objects that suddenly increased their speed, accelerating with incredible velocity. Moments later a second formation of identical objects flew into their field of vision.

The Great Flying Saucer Age was now in high gear, and few people realized that the Arnold sightings were *not* the curtain raisers to the era of UFOs. We have already seen how far back in history the sighting of strange and unidentified objects had been going on, but from 1947 on the every-now-and-then reports became a tremendous flood of day and night sightings.

World War II had produced its own rash of unidentified objects—formations of small silvery discs and black discs that crashed into the wings and fuselages of American heavy bombers on raids into Germany, especially during the raid of October 14, 1943, against the ball-bearing factories of Schweinfurt. On that mission hundreds of crewmen sighted the small silvery discs, barely a few inches in diameter, sweeping head-on at the B-17 bombers. They could be seen and heard colliding with the bombers and leaving indentations in the metal surfaces. No one ever understood what these discs were, where they came from, or what they were doing.

Pilots on both sides of the war were agitated by so-called foo fighters, brightly colored white, red, orange, blue, yellow, or green fiercely blazing balls of fire, that shot up from the earth or descended from higher altitude, racing wildly through formations, sometimes accompanying fighters and bombers with a crazy abandon. Each side thought the enemy was controlling a new type of weapon that sometimes appeared to interfere with the electrical systems of engines and aircraft, but it soon became obvious these were *not* weapons, and the Germans were as mystified as the Americans and the British, all of whom encountered these frustrating fireballs in both day and night missions. Then, several weeks before the tremendous air war came to a close in May 1945, the foo fighters vanished inexplicably. There was speculation that they were an electrical form of energy that somehow managed to "cross over" from a parallel continuum, race about madly, and then flash back into their own time and space. Most scientists ridiculed these theories, calling them supernatural nonsense, but when asked for a better explanation, the scientists could only shrug.

Between 1947 and today, *there have been several hundred thousand reported sightings of UFOs*, from people from every walk of life, from small farmers to scientists with elaborate instruments that could track a sparrow. The actual count of sightings could be in the millions. The uproar that accompanied the UFO reports initiated acrimonious debates, name-calling, skepticism, religious fervor, cults, and a smaller group of trained, experienced, capable technicians, scientists, engineers, and pilots whose word, until they reported sighting a UFO, was judged as unimpeachable. This group learned quickly *not* to report what they encountered in the skies. There is a huge wall of resistance on the part of officialdom—government, industry, airlines, scientists, engineers, and military—to accept UFOs as real.

People, insist the professionals, simply aren't very good at observing things. They cite mirages, the reflections that float ships, animals, people, entire cities, mountains, rivers, lakes, trees, *anything*, in the air. Few people understand that *mirage* means simply mirror image. Atmospheric conditions sometimes turn the skies into incredible mirrors that distort, expand, discolor, energize, flash, dart, float, displace, and do other strange and wonderful things to perfectly normal objects. They cause stationary lights to flicker, blink, wax, wane, shift colors, and then dance wildly about the sky. Do the observers have cameras? Camcorders? And have they recorded on film or tape these wonders of the sky?

If so, the resulting pictures, films, or videos are often greeted with derision. Cameras take excellent pictures of mirages and make them *seem* to be what the observers insist they really are—spacecraft, super aircraft, antigravity vessels.

It is true that many UFO sightings are of strange but absolutely natural phenomena. The grinding motion of faults in the earth create tremendous static discharges that can send balls of fire and showers of sparks bursting into the skies. Lightning tears downward, flashes in circles, and often shoots outward into space, looking like rockets racing at fabulous speeds away from the earth after some unexplained visitation.

Rockets ascend from well-known launching sites, creating huge pyrotechnic displays that can be seen for many hundreds of miles. Reflected even farther by inversion layers, these launchings inevitably bring on thousands of reports that are true as to the sighting and the fireworks but mistaken as to the source.

And once the hundreds of various satellites and booster rocket bodies have been hurled into orbit, they put on shows of their own. Many rockets are never intended for orbit, but on their way upstairs they release great streams of chemicals, which become excited by solar and atmospheric energies and radiate tremendous colors over thousands of miles of sky.

Military research on the ground and in the air also creates outlandish sights. Flares, rockets, searchlights, balloons, helicopters, special weapons, externally burning engines, helicopters with lights at the edge of their rotors that paint perfect circles in the air . . . this list frustrates the "believers" because the military won't release the details of what they're doing because the programs *are* secret and they are under no obligation to tell the world about what they're doing.

Yet, when you take away all of the sightings that may possibly have a natural explanation, there still remains thousands of notably unexplainable sightings, many by veteran observers, pilots, and other solid, sober citizens who have refused to reveal their sightings to the media. What follows are several of these startling reports. They have never before appeared in print of any kind.

UFO REPORTS

There is a document on file at the Air Force's Air University Research Studies Institute at Maxwell Air Force Base, Alabama, that contains military crew reports of sightings of inexplicable objects in flight. This document, like many others, has been classified for decades. Unlike many others referring to mysterious sightings by highly experienced military combat crews, this incident report is made available for the first time, anywhere, in these pages.

The incident report and a cover letter were released finally by transmission from the Research Studies Institute to Major General John A. Samford, Director of Intelligence, in Washington, D.C., in 1953. The letter reads:

Dear General Samford:

In view of recent news stories of lights seen over Japan the attached account may be of interest. The original is in the files of the Archives of the USAF Historical Division, Air University.

                    Sincerely yours,

                    Albert F. Simpson
                    Chief, USAF Historical Division

Here is the combat report document reprinted exactly as it was written on May 2, 1945. No changes have been made in the report that follows. I do not believe that what has remained hidden in classified files all these many years could be made even more bizarre and incredible.

HEADQUARTERS VII Bomber Command
APO #244
MISSION REPORT NO. 11-327
DATE: 2 May 1945

OBSERVATIONS: The crew of plane #616 over FALA ISLAND, TRUK ATOLL, at 021802Z observed 2 airborne objects at their 11,000 foot altitude changing from a cherry red to an orange, and to a white light which would die out and then become cherry red again. These objects were out on either wing and not within range of caliber .50 machine guns. Both followed the B-24 thru all types of evasive action. A B-24 took a course for GUAM and one of the pursuers dropped off at

021900Z after accompanying the B-24 for an hour.
The other continued to follow, never approaching
closer than 1,000 yards and speeding up when the
B-24 went thru the clouds to emerge on the other
side ahead of the B-24. In daylight it was seen to
be bright silver in color. As the B-24 let down at
GUAM, the pursuer took a course of 330 degrees
at 15,000 to 20,000 feet altitude at 022130Z. One
B-24 encountered eight intense flames light green
in color, one of which burst and hung at 5,000 feet
at 021013Z. There was no trail or warning until
the actual burst. A B-24 reported 9 to 10 red
tracer type trails of fire up to 5,000 feet. They
came in pairs and one pair came within 50 to 100
yards of the tail of the B-24 at 021010Z. Source of
each pair was at a different location.
[Source: Seventh Bomber Command Mission Reports, 742.332—8 February–16 May 1945]

That's the way it happened. The question, of course,
remains: *What* was encountered by the crews of those
four-engined B-24 bombers?

They weren't flown or lofted by any American forces.
They weren't Japanese, who were nowhere near Guam in
1945. Besides, U.S. research on this matter left the Japanese as baffled as anyone else.

All manner of combat records were scoured—the historical archives of the Air Force, including thousands of
combat crew debriefings and interrogations.

What happened was shocking. But to this day, no one
knows one iota more than you just read in the combat
report of the Seventh Bomber Command, except that, according to our best scientists and military experts, it was
impossible and therefore never could have happened.

What follows is a report from Robert A. Myers, for-
merly of the U.S. Army, that was never released to the
public, but was kept "extremely private for many years,

for reasons I hope you will judge as worthy of the long
silence. . . ."

From 1972 through 1976 I was stationed at Fort
Rucker as an instructor in the Army's Air Traffic
Control School. We had many civilian personnel
who worked for the Army as instructors; many of
them were retired pilots, or they had been air
traffic controllers with other services. I did special duty with three men who'd been former air
traffic controllers; now we worked as a team in a
secret radar laboratory. After a while we became
close enough to talk to one another about past
events you'd never say that might get on official
records.

My eyebrows went up when in a flat, matter-
of-fact level of conversation, as though it were the
most common thing in their official duty lives,
they eased into a conversation about a sighting
and encounter with a UFO. Russell Boyce was the
man closest to the event (for want of a better
word). It was what you'd call one of the worst-
kept secrets at his base. It seemed just about
everyone knew what had happened, but everything was kept strictly off the record. Please keep
in mind I'm talking about highly skilled and long-
experienced technicians. Nothing would faze
these guys.

They had all worked together at a military
airfield in Arizona, and at this time Boyce had
been the Watch Supervisor on the duty shift.
Now, Boyce was more than a radar technician
and an air traffic controller. He'd been a pilot in
the powerful Republic P-47 Thunderbolt fighter,
which was a handful for any man. When the second world war ended he was swept up in the RIF
[Reduction In Force] and he opted to yield his
commission as an officer and remain in the Air
Force as an enlisted man working in air traffic

control centers. That was a pretty common thing to do at that time. Guys who were colonels one day would show up the next morning with sergeant stripes on their arms and glad to have them.

The "event" happened sometime about 1952 or 1953. As they explained what had happened, they—including Boyce—were on duty, with Boyce running the shift, when someone spotted some huge objects in the sky. The exact word was *huge*. Whatever these things were, they approached the airfield and then came to a stop in midair, at "extreme altitude"—again, those were their words—and they remained unmoving, "like they were covering the sky."

The people at the base just flipped. This wasn't one of those flash-in-the-pan sightings. I mean, as Boyce emphasized, they were *all* watching the objects that remained in sight and still holding their position in the sky. That alone is a direct tip-off that something *very* unusual was going on, way beyond just seeing these objects. Because at high altitude you do have very strong winds, and for these objects to remain in one position over the ground below—a fixed hover position—they *had* to be expending some kind of thrust or force to keep the wind from blowing them from their position. At those altitudes, especially if you get into a jetstream, you face winds anywhere from one to three hundred miles an hour, and sometimes greater. But there were these huge objects, defying every natural law that Boyce and the others understood.

This went on for several minutes until someone got his mental wheels going. The base maintained a force of North American F-86 Sabre swept-wing jet fighters, and their commander ordered a couple of the fighters to "get up there and see what the hell is going on."

Easier said than done. The '86 was a hot

airplane and the pilots climbed at full power. They kept climbing until the air was so thin their control surfaces became sloppy and their engines began flaming out from lack of oxygen.

By now everybody was listening in to the radio calls from the F-86 pilots. They were a pretty steady bunch of people, most of them combat veterans, and it took a lot to shake up these guys who had spent a lot of time in the air with other people trying to kill them. That sort of gives you a Rock-of-Gibraltar frame of mind.

The pilots, fighting for control of their airplanes, confirmed that the objects, whatever they were, were "huge," and that they had reached the absolute ceiling of the F-86s and could go no higher. They also reported that the things were still so far above them they couldn't get close enough to really make out the kind of detail they wanted to see.

At this time Boyce was in the control tower. Every tower during this period, when Operation Bluebook to investigate UFO sightings was in full swing, had special cameras to try to catch on film whatever appeared in the sky. Boyce and his crew shot their pictures and logged every detail they had in the tower record books.

After the fighters came whistling down with some very bewildered and frustrated pilots, a group of security people moved in—*fast.*

The camera kept in the tower was secured and sealed to prevent tampering or removal. When the security people (never clearly identified beyond obvious high authority to do as they pleased, that authority coming from levels far above those at this airfield) moved in, they dismantled the camera mount, removed the camera and its film, and also seized the tower logs! At the same time the F-86 pilots who'd flown the attempted interception were taken to a secured room; they were first asked a horde of questions, and then officially "debriefed." In effect, they were told to clam up. Just plain keep their mouths closed about the matter. The security people "vigorously discouraged" them from any talking on the whole affair, and warned that the consequences of breaking silence could be severe. That doesn't go over very well with veteran combat pilots, but the F-86 jocks also recognized when the hammer was coming down.

Apparently, because he was in the middle of it all, Russell Boyce really got the shaft. His official notice of what went on, his detailed log entry, for some reason was held against him. His two colleagues said flatly that, in some way, Boyce's records were "flagged," and he might just as well kiss good-bye any promotions he certainly expected in the future.

So I asked Russell Boyce, directly, in a one-on-one conversation, if this really was true. I can only assume that by now, years later, Boyce was so burned by the pressure on him that he didn't much give a damn what higher authority might do to him. He said his two friends had told it just like it was, and the sightings and subsequent attempted interception, and especially his knowledge of the whole matter, followed him around in his career like a dark and angry shadow. Notations were made in his records that certainly did block his promotions; plus, he added, a "whole bunch of other things" took place that were pretty rotten.

"I'll tell you right now, Myers," he said seriously, "that if you ever get into a situation like that one, you'll be well advised to find out what the people on top really want you to do. You, in the meantime, don't do anything to prove or dis-

prove anything, understand? You just dummy up
and you don't do anything you're not specifically
ordered to do. If I'd had smarts then, if I knew
then what was going to happen to me, I would
never have touched that camera, standing order
from Bluebook or not. And if anybody asks you
what you saw, you tell them you saw some really
weird clouds, and you let it go at that."

I don't know what else happened, when I
wasn't around, that is, but those three men would
never again discuss the matter with me. It was
done with, *period.*

Jeff E. Brewton of Lompoc, California, sighted mysterious lights in the Lompoc area in March 1990. He's an
experienced observer of many types of aircraft and extremely meticulous about the details of anything unusual
he might encounter. Like many of the experienced and
reliable people who encounter "unexplainable" things in
the air, he states what happened, in detail, and stops short
of drawing conclusions based on incomplete data, which
makes his report all the more meaningful.

Our daughter, Lezlee, manages our video store
and had something she needed to do one evening
and asked me to close for her. Aimee Powers, our
clerk, was running the store and closed at 8:00
P.M. At 8:10 she finished her last-minute work. . . .
I walked her to the front of the store and as she
exited, I looked south to the hills about a mile
away. There, low on the horizon, were four large
white lights that immediately caught my attention
because of their unusual appearance. Turning to
Aimee to get her attention, I realized she had
already walked about 25 feet, turned right, and
disappeared around the side of the building heading for her car. My first impression was that the
lights belonged to hot-air balloons, but that was

quickly rejected because the flame on hot-air balloons is not white, and the light shining through
the balloons at night is affected by the color of the
material or design. Balloons are also noisy.

These [lights] did not have the brightness of
landing lights. After watching for what seemed
several minutes the lights appeared to start moving very, very slowly toward me. Three lights
formed a triangle while the fourth was out a short
distance. It reminded me of a fighter plane formation with the fourth plane on the left side.

The lights seemed to come directly toward
me for maybe five minutes before turning slowly
on a heading toward Vandenberg Air Force Base,
a heading of about 300 degrees. The lights seemed
to come within a quarter mile and slowly, very
slowly, passed out of sight.

There were no red or green lights showing
[as is common on aircraft flying at night], nor
was a strobe visible. I tried to see a silhouette
against the sky but was unsuccessful. At the closest point a very low hum could be heard. The
estimated altitude was less than 500 feet above
ground. Speed was the strangest aspect. The
lights slowly passed at an estimated speed of 10
to 15 miles per hour. From the size of the lights
and the distance apart, if this was one aircraft, it
would be large . . . like a 747.

Yes, I know planes can't fly that slowly except for the Harrier or whatever can hover because of its vertical takeoff and landing capability, and no, it wasn't a helicopter; the sounds and
the size were wrong. Lompoc is under the glide
path for Vandenberg Air Force Base and since the
runway was lengthened for shuttle work, we get
many large planes shooting touch-and-goes. It is
common to see P-3s, C-130s, C-141s, and B-52s
plus an assortment of fighters and other planes

approach Vandenberg, so locally we have some
idea of the sounds and speeds of the approach.

There is still a sense of unreality about the
sighting. . . .

Joe Ficarotta is a highly qualified observer of anything that flies. For several decades he headed many projects involving photographing and filming missiles, huge
rockets, and "other targets" at Cape Canaveral in Florida,
where he began in 1956 as a motion picture cameraman
with RCA. He went on to become the director of motion
pictures and still photography for the Air Force at the
Cape, which was the launch complex for the Air Force
Missile Test Center. He continued this line of work with
the Technicolor Corporation, producing motion picture and
video productions for the Air Force and for NASA. His
experience in this line of work makes him one of the most
qualified observers of objects in flight.

It was a UFO sighting.

Not one of those "I saw a strange light in the
night sky" sightings which account for many
false UFO reports. This happened in *broad daylight* with a clear, cloudless sky, about two
o'clock in the afternoon. I was enjoying a week-
end swim with the wife and kids in our backyard
pool. . . . Suddenly, something very unusual appeared in the sky from behind a clump of trees on
the east end of our lot. It was about 45 degrees
above the horizon, traveling from north to south
at an estimated speed of 300 to 400 miles per
hour. It appeared to be a huge, metallic object
about 150 to 200 feet long, shaped somewhat like
a cigar.

*It had no wings, tail surfaces, or visible en-
gine nacelles.* There was no engine noise as it
quietly, steadily flew in a straight line across the
sky heading south. It was in my line of sight for

about 15 seconds, with no obstacles in my way during that time. There was enough time to scrutinize it carefully and note the details of the craft.

I noticed seams along the side facing me, indicating a manufacturing process of some kind. There was also a small pod attached to the craft near the front, somewhat like the pods attached to the rockets in our space program. It had no windows or ports that I could see, and the shape of it tapered down smaller toward the rear of the craft.

The front and rear surfaces appeared to be flat, defying conventional aerodynamic fuselage designs. There were markings on the object but they were not decipherable. They resembled ancient cuneiform or Egyptian hieroglyphics; nothing like I have ever seen before. Suspecting I may have been experiencing a grand hallucination, I quickly called the attention of my family to the craft and they verified what I had seen. Whatever it was, it was there and did traverse across the sky in our full view. . . .

John M. Fitzpatrick, a fighter pilot ordered to scramble for an intercept, presents a "sidereal viewpoint" of an encounter with a UFO that *he never saw*. This incident raises the serious question of why some people can see objects and others cannot, although they are all pilots, competent observers, and searching for the same target. This episode definitely requires further investigation.

In the spring of 1950 I was an Air Force pilot assigned as an experimental test pilot in the Fighter Section of the Flight Test Division at Wright-Patterson Air Force Base. On a Saturday morning I was conducting landing tests on an F-80 [jet fighter] at Wright Field. This was during the time that "Flying Saucers" were first in the news. I received a call from Wright tower asking if I had enough fuel to check a report from a pair of National Guard P-51 pilots flying out of Vandalia (Dayton Municipal Airport). I said yes. Since we hád only four-channel VHF radios without a common frequency the Guard pilots and I had to communicate through the tower operators.

I located the two P-51s at about 15,000 feet near Dayton and pulled up in formation with them. The flight leader kept pointing forward and up. The tower operator told me that he was pointing at a large circular object several miles ahead and several thousand feet higher. He said he and his wingman had pursued it for some time but weren't fast enough to catch it, so they asked if a jet was available. The problem was that I couldn't see anything out there! I dropped back behind the flight leader so that I was looking exactly where he was looking. Still nothing. According to the tower operator, the P-51 pilots were getting quite angry that I could not see what they saw. Eventually I had to break off and return to Wright Field because of fuel.

After I got on the ground I called the National Guard operations office and talked to both pilots. There is no question that they believed that they had seen what they claimed to have seen and made derogatory comments about my eyesight. Since all of our conversations in the air had been on tower frequency a number of other pilots had also looked for the "flying saucer" but no one else saw it either.

I do not believe that the P-51 pilots were making up a hoax. They both "saw" something that no one else could see. Since then I have never ruled out the possibility of "flying saucers," although I have never seen one.

The following report comes from a man with extraordinary technological, scientific, combat, investigations, and pilot credentials. It has an extraordinary resemblance to that reported by ex-test pilot John Fitzpatrick. Only under the writer's condition of anonymity is this material released for the first time.

The time was 2200 hours on a night of crystal-clear visibility in mid-December 1952. Air Force 8073, a B-50 Superfortress bomber, eased onto the runway stretching 10,500 feet ahead of us at Hunter Air Force Base in Savannah, Georgia. On board was a SAC (Strategic Air Command) "Select-Lead Crew," the best of the best in SAC, made up of World War II combat veterans. The one exception was myself; I was a staff sergeant (everyone else was high officer rank) and I'd been in the Korean War.

As a Select-Lead Crew we were briefed (like the others) on a preselected target in Russia. It was a one-way mission where you hit your target and, assuming you survived the strike, you returned as far as you could to friendly territory. If you could make it, you landed. If not, you flew until you exhausted your fuel and then we were all to bail out and hope for the best.

When we took off on the target missions we were usually 40,000 pounds over gross weight. Losing an engine on the takeoff roll usually meant a lot of other crews watching our airplane would be treated to the sight of a spectacular fireball and the cremation of everyone inside the airplane. On this flight we were in training, the air was cold, and the B-50 launched smartly into the night. This was a proficiency mission, bombing selected "targets" and performing a night refueling with a tanker. We were southbound to Mac-Dill Air Force Base near Tampa, Florida, climbing to 25,000 feet and then, after passing over Mac-

Dill, taking up a westerly course over the Gulf of Mexico to Randolph Air Force Base in Texas.

Our bomb bays were modified so that we could carry one hell of a "Fat Man" nuke in the front bay and a bag of fuel in the rear bay. Like the B-29 that preceded this model, you still nearly froze to death above 25,000 feet where the outside air temperature was commonly forty degrees or more below zero. About halfway across the Gulf our radar operator began calibrating his system to provide vectors to Randolph. He picked up a target and, taking it to be a ship, routinely reported, "Target at 12 o'clock, 60 miles."

A moment later he exclaimed, "Hey, this thing's moving pretty fast! Target is now 12 o'clock, 50 miles—No! Make that 48, uh, 45 miles! Holy Jesus, this thing is *airborne!*"

He called the aircraft commander. "Sir, check target at 12 o'clock, 40 miles."

"Roj, we're looking," came the reply. Then, "No joy."

Strangely, this was to be the only response from the front office. Pilots given that kind of call don't lapse into silence, but ours did.

The radarman called out again, "Target's now 12 o'clock, 30 miles, coming *fast!*"

The flight deck remained silent.

Barely seconds later the radarman called out, "Check bogey at 12 o'clock, 20 miles."

Then, only seconds later, his strained voice sang out, "Target moving towards one o'clock now, *five* miles."

Silence from up front.

Seconds later, a streak with the intensity of a neon light, but brighter and bluer, but painless to my night-conditioned eyes, pierced the night sky on the right side of the aircraft. It flashed by and disappeared aft. Slightly below our altitude, it was visible from the right gunner's position, a plastic blister, for not more than a half-second.

The leading and trailing edge of the "streak" was blunt; its distance from our flight path anywhere from 600 to 1,200 feet, and its height (if my distance judgment was correct) between 30 to 60 feet. At the incredible speed involved—it moved 60 miles in 45 seconds, which computes to 4,800 miles per hour—coupled with our speed of 200 miles per hour, it resulted in a closure rate of more than 5,000 miles per hour. Almost impossible to accurately assess shape like that. However, I've looked at a lot of targets in my time and my perception was strongly of a tubular shape.

We heard nothing over the sound of our own engines.

After all these years some very hard questions persist. We were all top of the line as crew. We all had top-secret clearance. We were handpicked.

Question 1: Why did no one report seeing this object?

Question 2: Why didn't the aircraft commander take evasive action? This object couldn't have been more than a quarter mile off our right wing. This is near-miss country! And over England, this pilot once raised absolute hell over a British Lancaster bomber nearly a mile away.

Question 3: Why no shock wave from this object? It was close enough and fast enough to have rocked us back on our heels.

Question 4: How could a ground-tracking radar pick up an object in flight? Initially, the radarman even thought he was tracking a ship on the surface of the Gulf.

Question 5: Why was the cockpit utterly silent on the event? The pilots even ceased acknowledging the reports of the radar operator.

Question 6 (which may fit the pilots): *I* saw the object. Why didn't I report it? I could have reported it afterward. But then, I had a previous experience that kept me cautious about reporting anything out of line. I was once grilled by an Intelligence Team in Japan for reporting flak 10,000 feet *above* our bombing altitude over North Korea. I knew it was flak; I just assumed our Electronic Countermeasures was doing a good job of messing up enemy radar, but it was *very* obvious by the line of questioning that they weren't the slightest bit interested in flak. Add to this that after the blazing neonlike streak shot past us, the radarman never said another word regarding the incident. He flat clammed up and I have always suspected he was silenced on the issue.

So I was left with speculations trailing after an unquestioned radar tracking and visual sighting of something glowing brilliantly and moving in either level flight or climbing—that no one would even acknowledge. Did the front office guys flying that B-50 maintain silence to protect their security clearances? That could be.

Or, and I'm still in the speculation mode, did the pilots ever *see* the object? It's unthinkable that with all those reports from the radarman, they *didn't* look.

Still speculating, I have always wondered whether whatever intelligence controls or operates these things also has the capability to cloak the visual perception of their presence.

Or . . . and I know this gets a bit hairy, is it possible that only certain people can see these objects?

I don't know. The official silence went so far that the crew *never* discussed the matter, even with one another.

Somebody sure slammed the door shut on what happened.

The following details are from a report, astonishing and shocking because of the terseness and technical details, that was made available for this book and transmitted privately. The full report, couched in terms of hypotheses for personal security reasons, is unfortunately much too lengthy to be presented here. It is filled with supporting documentation, dates, names, places, and other evidence.

The individual who prepared this report is the captain of a jumbo-jet airliner that routinely flies all over the world with several hundred passengers aboard. During his career he has flown perhaps 170 different types of aircraft, many demanding extremely high levels of skill and competence, and he has flown in areas both well known and extremely remote encompassing more than fifty countries. He holds world records for many flights. He is also the only pilot to have been granted *Every* airman certificate by the U.S. Federal Aviation Administration.

Here are excerpts from that long and detailed report.

One of the lead investigators, when in Vietnam as a member of a Special Forces Investigative Team, went in to retrieve what could be removed from a B-52 that had been forced down by a UFO, and all occupants of the B-52 killed. Communications had been received from the B-52 before it went down to the effect that it was "under attack by a UFO . . . a large light . . ." The aircraft was found in heavy jungle. There was no swath indicative of a crash landing. Only the bottom of the aircraft showed damage, but there was no damage to the underside of the engine pods. Generally the aircraft was fully intact, *but the entire crew had been mutilated. . . .*

Our source states without qualification that the U.S. government has an ongoing project "dealing specifically

with UFOs and captured aliens." Supporting documentation for this area was not provided because it is still under
security classification. This same report states that "people
who had experienced close encounters" with UFOs "were
isolated" from the mainstream of their normal lives. Again,
supporting documentation was not provided for security
reasons. . . .

Report 13 on UFOs was in a "diplomatic pouch under
lock and key system. . . . Standard diplomatic courier's
pouch marked American Embassy Couriers, contained
Pouch Serial Number JL327Delta . . . [marked with] code
red security precautions . . . observe all code red measures.
Analysis required immediately. . . . Report identified
further as AFSN 2246-3 . . . Top Secret Need To Know
Only Crypto Clearance 14 Required."

"People who it was determined had genuine close
encounters . . . were moved in the middle of the night by
Air Force personnel and relocated to various sites in the
midwest and northwest parts of the United States. In
many cases these people experienced physical ailments
from exposure to various types of radiation."

In October 1953, an Ohio farmer and family observed
"a round ball of fire [hovering] over field where boy and
dog had run to . . . heard boy screaming for help . . . father
fired several rounds from shotgun [when] he saw his son
being carried away by what looked like little men, into this
huge fiery looking object. . . . [Later] they found dog, its
head was crushed but no sign of boy or any other footprints. . . . Father immediately called police. . . . Within 48
hours the Air Force made the determination that the family
was to be relocated. . . . The mother was in shock and had
to go through a great deal of psychotherapy and depro-
gramming as did father."

"Report [gives] clear indication of . . . human mutila-

tions, most notably a case witnessed by Air Force personnel in which . . . Sgt. EE-6 J. P. Lovette was observed being
taken captive aboard what appeared to be a UFO at the
White Sands Missile Test Range in New Mexico. This
abduction took place in March of 1956 at about 0300 local
and was witnessed by Major William Cunningham of the
U.S.A.F. Missile Test Command near Holloman Air Force
Base. . . . Major Cunningham heard Sgt. Lovette scream . . .
saw Sgt. Lovette being dragged into a . . . silvery disc-like
object which hovered in the air approximately 15 to 20 feet
. . . a long snake-like object [was] wrapped about the
sergeant's legs and was dragging him to the craft. . . .
Cunningham observed the disc going up into the sky very
quickly. . . . The search for Lovette was continued for three
days at the end of which his nude body was found approximately 10 miles downrange. The body had been mutilated;
the tongue had been removed from lower portion of the
jaw. An incision had been made just under the tip of the
chin and extended all the way back to the esophagus and
larynx. He had been emasculated and his eyes had been
removed. Also, his anus had been removed and there were
comments in the report on the apparent surgical skill of the
removal of these items including the genitalia. . . . the
system had been completely drained of blood and there
was no vascular collapse due to death by bleeding. . . ."

"Photos [of aliens from UFOs] showed an alien being
on an autopsy table which is a metal table with runnels
and traps underneath to trap fluid and feces. Body appeared to be a little short of four feet. Table was about
seven feet. No clothing on body, no genitalia, body completely heterous, head was rounded cranium, slightly en-
larged, eyes almond shaped, slits where nose would be,
extremely small mouth, receding chin line, holes where
ears would be. Photo was taken at angle, side view, looking at body from 45° elevation, left hand was visible, head
was facing to left, body was right to left position (head on
right, feet on left), eyes were closed, appeared oriental-

looking and almond shaped, left hand slightly longer than normal, wrist coming down just about two to three inches above the knees. Wrists appeared to be articulated in a fashion that allowed a double joint with three digit fingers. Wrist was very slender. There was no thumb. A palm was almost nonexistent. The three fingers were direct extension from the wrist. . . ."

"Photo taken of three live aliens. Very clear photo, aliens standing against white tile wall, looking confused as if they had been shoved, were looking in different directions. . . .

"U.S. Air Force relocation personnel (for persons involved in close encounters) were referred to in the report as 'Men in Black.'

"Major Cunningham was initially accused of murdering Sgt. Jonathan P. Lovette. Charges were later dropped. . . .

"Lead source of data was from individual with service at RAF Security Services Command, RAF Chicksands. . . .

"Report stated that there were seventeen different extraterrestrial species accounted for. . . .

"The report discussed civilian and military personnel who had been terminated 'to eliminate potentially dangerous elements to the national security.' . . ."

End of report. There are times when the writer says, *Let the reader decide.* This is one of those times.

Investigations of UFO sightings and reported landings are an ongoing activity by government, corporate, and private groups throughout the United States. Each year, or more frequently if "new material of immediate nature" is obtained, members of such groups, along with outside researchers brought in by invitation, assemble to compare notes and review photography, video, and film and any other data pertaining to UFO matters.

One such group gathered in June 1992 on the campus

of the University of Wyoming at Laramie under the auspices of the Rocky Mountain UFO Conference. The assembly was hosted by Leo Sprinkle and June Parnell.

Scott H. Colborn, international director of the Fortean Research Center, a group of highly experienced scientists, investigators, pilots, and others, represented members from across the United States. The purpose of the conference was to update and cross-reference sightings, reported landings, and other activities related to UFO phenomena and to present this material for dissemination to and input from researchers. Colborn reported that Dr. Steven Greer presented an unexpected videotape. "Dr. Greer," wrote Colborn, "showed a videotape that purportedly was sent to Bob Oechsler of Edgewater, Maryland. The video is of a landed disc in Canada. The date of the landing was August 18, 1991. The source who sent the tape to Oechsler is using the name 'Guardian.' As the tape plays, it is dark and you see a disc in the right of the frame with bright light displayed on the ground around the disc. There's a red flashing strobe light on top, and Greer said it was flashing at seven times a second. In the left of the frame are what look like flares burning. I estimate that the flares were about 30–50 feet away and to the left of the disc. The photographer is recording as he/she walks toward the disc and then walks to his/her right, at which point the tape stops. It's hard to make estimates, but I would guess that the person(s) shooting the videotape got about 100–150 feet away from the disc before moving to the right.

"I recently discussed the matter by phone with Oechsler. He believes it is not a hoax. He has found the site, has been there, and has collected soil samples which are being analyzed by the University of Maryland; he, Oechsler, had spoken with 'eyewitnesses.' Oechsler said the event took place near Ottawa, Canada. He said it was a 'Canadian operation,' and the military got there three minutes after the disc had departed. It is either a really good fake [the videotape] or it is sensational news. We are continuing our own investigations. . . ."

4
"A Terrifying Sight"

It was a perfect night for crossing the Pacific Ocean. A full moon cast a silvery glow on a cloud deck at fifteen thousand feet above the ocean, transforming the world into the surface of another planet with ghostly gleams of light.

It was the night of April 9, 1984. A Japan Air Lines cargo flight, a Boeing 747, was en route from Tokyo to the United States with a planned stopover in Anchorage, Alaska. In the Boeing, call sign Japan Air Three Six, Captain Charles L. McDade relaxed in the flight deck's left seat, the cargo liner riding like silk with computerized autopilot systems flying the airplane flawlessly. To McDade it was another beautiful, comfortable milk run. He was sixty years old and he'd been flying for forty-one years. Before he took the captain's seat of the commercial 747, McDade had spent many years flying all kinds of bombers in a military career, and in that time he'd earned the reputation of a "pretty calm cookie." It's an accolade a pilot gets only by surviving when the going gets rough. McDade was that kind of man: solid, experienced, skilled, reliable. He was the kind of pilot you'd fly anywhere with.

It had been forty-five minutes since McDade had advanced the thrust levers of the heavy 747 to begin accelerating down the runway of Tokyo's major airport. Then began the long steady climb to cruising altitude, and they were well east of Tokyo, approximately 180 miles off the Japanese coast.

The time was 2306 hours—six minutes past 11:00 P.M. local time.

Then *it* happened.

McDade and his crew stared aghast at the cloud deck five miles below them, at what they described as "a terrifying sight" in that ghostly but unquestionable light from the moon.

It looked like the beginning of World War III.

The cloud deck seemed to bulge. At first McDade and his first officer couldn't believe that. But the bulge continued to expand, and now it was casting a shadow on the cloud deck, proof positive that *something* was lunging up through the solid cloud layer.

A monstrous mushroom cloud was booming upward into the night sky. The pilots had never seen anything like it in real life before. They knew instantly what they were seeing. They'd all watched newsreels and combat and military films of the great mushroom clouds boiling upward, first from Hiroshima, then from Nagasaki. But those were firecrackers compared with the mushroom clouds that erupted from hydrogen bombs of twenty million tons explosive power and more.

And what they were seeing now dwarfed even the mightiest test explosion of a hydrogen bomb.

The mushroom cloud expanded as it rose until it was more than two hundred miles in diameter. It shot upward from fourteen thousand feet to sixty thousand feet in no more than two minutes.

The pilots were convinced that they were seeing the explosion of a thermonuclear warhead beneath the cloud layer that was now thrusting up into the stratosphere.

Immediately McDade was on his radio to Anchorage Center.

"Anchorage . . . *Mayday! Mayday!* . . ." The international emergency call *always* gets immediate attention. "Anchorage Radio, this is Japan Air Three Six—do you read me? Over!"

Anchorage responded immediately. "Japan Air Three Six, Anchorage Radio, loud and clear. Go ahead, sir."

"Japan Air Three Six . . . we have a . . ." McDade

hesitated a moment, seeking the right words. "A . . . round ball cloud, looks like a nuclear explosion, only . . . there was no fireball and there was no lighting. but the cloud was there, very definitely. . . . the cloud continues to explode like a great big cloud . . . easy to see it . . . the moon is behind it and it expanded very rapidly. . . . I turned off course to get away from it as much as possible. We are on one hundred percent oxygen just as a precaution. . . ."

That meant that the flight crew had all donned emergency oxygen masks and were breathing directly from safe, sealed systems.

"Everything is normal as far as our operations are concerned. Over."

"Japan Air Three Six, Anchorage, roger, roger . . ."

Captain Charles L. McDade and his crew weren't the only pilots that night to stare in mixed awe and horror at a sight that was almost too much to believe. The cloud kept boiling into the night sky until it seemed to be miles above their cruising altitude, and it continued to expand outward in all directions until the distance it covered stretched farther than from New York to Washington, D.C.

Then upper atmospheric windows and other forces still not understood began to shred the cloud. It lost its mushroom shape and spread widely in different directions.

But in Japan the tension was cable-taut. Two other airliners called in, their crews also disbelieving and clearly shocked. McDade's call to Anchorage was monitored by Japanese air traffic control; keeping tabs on planes flying along the lower limits of Soviet territory was a standard practice. But the Japanese did more than simply listen. They ordered a powerful McDonnell-Douglas F-4J Phantom II fighter-bomber into the air to get to the cloud as quickly as possible. The powerful fighter went directly into the cloud so that collector devices aboard the Phantom might collect elements of the cloud or whatever was within its roiling upsurge.

The first thing everybody wanted to confirm was

whether that cloud *had* been the result of some gigantic thermonuclear blast, either on the surface of the ocean or even deep beneath the water, sending the fireball to the surface and then spewing forth the cloud. But a hydrogen bomb would explode a fireball anywhere from five to fifteen miles in diameter, and that is only the fireball. The light from such an explosion, more than 150 million degrees at its center, is more than enough to turn night into a devastating glare that makes bright sunlight gloomy by comparison.

No one saw any such light. Both Japanese and American teams interrogated the crews of *four* airliners that had seen and reported the cloud as it boiled up from the Pacific Ocean. Then they scoured the airliners, as they did the F-4J for any traces of residual radioactive particles, which would undoubtedly be present in such an incredible phenomenon.

No radioactivity. None. Bewilderment grew.

McDade's first thought at the sight of the cloud had remained with him. He told investigators that his instinctive reaction to the sight was that a Soviet missile had exploded, perhaps from a test, perhaps as an accident. After all, McDade knew the cloud was just about five hundred miles from Soviet territory, and to the north and northwest there were huge Soviet missile installations.

The Soviets appeared to be as bedeviled as anyone else.

McDade found the growing mystery difficult to understand—and to accept. As he had explained, his first thought was that a Soviet missile had detonated. "So I turned tail and ran," he said. "It was tremendous. I've never seen anything like it except in newsreels."

The mystery deepened. The official positions of Japanese, Soviet, and American governments were bland—so much so that investigators of military affairs and natural phenomena soon concluded that the lameness of the explanations and the lack of any serious investigation spoke volumes about the manner in which the entire episode was being passed off with a wave of the official hand.

One of the first "possible explanations," from doubting-Thomas scientists who'd heard the reports but little specific detail, was that it *might* have been some sort of titanic underwater volcanic blast.

That shouldn't be too difficult to check out. After all, anti-submarine warfare systems maintained by the United States can just about detect a whale hiccuping a thousand miles or more from any one of its underwater detection devices, which stay alert around the clock to keep track of Soviet submarines. What had *they* detected?

Officially, nothing. ASW (anti-submarine warfare) systems are covered by *very* high military security, and the U.S. Navy wasn't about to say anything that might give the Soviets even the smallest edge in better understanding how our systems worked.

Almost at once there was an outcry of "aha!" from various scientific circles. Of course it had to be volcanic, or subterranean volcanic, or lower ocean volcanic. It had to be, since nothing else in the entire lexicon of science fit the situation.

Enter Daniel A. Walker, the leading geophysicist of the University of Hawaii at Manoa, in Honolulu. Walker not only tackled scientific research, he moved along the blurred borderline between academic research and military interests. He operated a complex system of hydrophones—reliable underwater devices that detect and report on unusual gurgles, blasts, moans, and other sounds from the ocean bottom. Walker's interests lay far beyond shifting mud or underwater shelf slides, or even volcanic action, for he was also under contract to the Air Force Office of Scientific Research and represented the United States Arms Control and Disarmament Agency. Those are powerful credentials.

Walker's studies seemed to confirm the theory that the massive mushroom cloud—in physical form, outline, and ascent rate virtually identical to the same form of cloud that would result from the blast of a hydrogen bomb—was really the aftereffect of deep underwater volcanic activity. That was the explanation the government was hoping for.

Some of the instrumentation banks tended by Walker were supersensitive to more than underwater volcanic venting or the gastronomical outgassing of whales. They were set to detect and record nuclear weapons being exploded underwater. In short, we were keeping open our underwater ears for anything the Soviets, French, British, or Chinese—or anyone else—might be testing within the concealment offered by the sea.

"If there had been an underwater nuclear explosion," Walker explained, "our instruments would have picked up the unique sound pattern we know accompanies a single large explosion."

There was some pretty hearty backslapping in the Pentagon when Walker and his team confirmed it was *not* an underwater nuclear explosion. It *had* to be an underwater volcanic eruption. Never mind that in all the history of studying explosions beneath the sea, and in all the decades of monitoring subterranean volcanic activity, there had *never* been anything encountered like the mushroom cloud eruption of April 9, 1984.

Government scientists went after the volcanic explosion theory with all the zeal of hounds pursuing a bleeding fox. And they really seemed to have the scent, because on April 8 and again the day the cloud was sighted not only had the ocean boiled violently from furious underwater activity, but the hydrophone-detection system confirmed that something of tremendous power had taken place in the deep ocean—with the best guesses pointing to an enormous underwater volcanic eruption. This event could have produced a massive gas bubble tearing upward to the surface and, still furiously hot and compact, now freed of ocean-water pressure, racing upward to equalize that pressure. Voilà! One massive cloud booming into the stratosphere explained—finally.

Walker said, "The hydrophone recordings really suggested that the cloud was merely debris thrown up by an active submarine volcano in the area. And when I found out that pilots from the Japanese Maritime Safety Agency had seen a volcano near Iwo Jima erupting a month earlier, I thought for sure we had identified the mystery source."

All the loose pieces had come together and the entire affair should have gone neatly into the record books as one more normal natural phenomenon.

Well, science is often dead wrong.

Daniel Walker is a painstaking researcher and, from his performance records, it seems certain he takes nothing for granted and tracks down every detail to its last iota of possible evidence. The volcano that had brought so many sighs of relief to end the mystery was soon identified as the Kaitoku Seamount. Its formation is quite common in the Pacific Ocean near Japan. Walker clearly identified it on ocean charts, pinpointing its location as about eighty miles north of the island of Iwo Jima.

The solution seemingly at hand deflated like a pricked balloon, because the Kaitoku Seamount lies nine hundred miles southwest of where the tremendous cloud had boomed upward through the cloud deck.

Troubled by the distance measurements, Walker then turned to meteorological charts he obtained from the National Climatic Data Center. These charts would give him a record of the winds at all different altitudes for April 8 and 9.

"The charts showed without a doubt that I was totally wrong," Walker announced. "The winds were blowing to the southeast those days, away from the mushroom cloud's position. Kaitoku's activity and the cloud sighting were purely coincidental."

Walker was now face-to-face with a most perplexing conundrum. Without any specific answer to identify the startling cloud, he had no choice but to offer what had always been an obvious—and ominous—possibility.

"There are only two known phenomena—man-made explosions and natural volcanic eruptions occurring directly beneath the cloud—that could produce a cloud that size, rising as fast as it did with the shape it had. The Wake hydrophones would have detected a local submarine disturbance and didn't, which leaves us in the uncomfortable position of not knowing *what* produced the cloud."

What kind of energy can produce a cloud of that size, energy, and rate of ascent?

The most obvious answer is a huge hydrogen bomb. What Walker and many other scientists familiar with thermonuclear weapons feared was that what had happened as a singular event could happen again, but this time with multiple monster clouds booming up from the oceans to fill the skies.

The question of how to prevent such a horrifying mistake haunted Walker and other scientists. A natural phenomenon, *if* that is what the cloud was, could precipitate an all-out nuclear strike by one country convinced it was being attacked by an enemy.

"There are people sitting with their fingers on the proverbial red buttons," Walker mused unhappily, "and I'd sure hate for one of them to misinterpret the appearance of a strange mushroom cloud."

He added that he was more than perplexed about the official offhandedness about what had happened. "This thing could be solved if the right kind of minds are put to bear on the problem. I'm quite nervous about this thing just being forgotten."

A man long experienced in both mass destruction and exotic weapons systems, Lieutenant Colonel Thomas Beardon at the time the cloud exploded was already retired from active army duty, but had remained in weapons development as a weapons analyst for a major contractor with the military.

Beardon referred to a more specific statement by Walker about the geographical coordinates of the mushroom cloud: "Because of the location [of the mushroom cloud] you can't help but think of the Russians. If there's no nice, neat, happy explanation, we're forced into some scary explanations."

Colonel Beardon shared the same mind-set with Walker. Beardon has long been a well-known and tireless researcher into weaponry most people not only have never heard of, but can't even imagine. One of those weaponry fields is what Beardon describes as "scalar electromagnetics."

What scalar electromagnetics does, explains the colonel, is transmit two or more powerful electromagnetic beams at a specific, distant point, set so that they will intersect in a specific location. The beams, where they intersect, are almost a bi-dimensional weapon, because they can either produce enormous amounts of outward exploding energy or they can drain energy from that specific location. Nature abhors a vacuum, and if you create an energy vacuum on the surface of a world where energy is constant and of tremendous, constantly shifting magnitude, that energy will rush into the "energy hole" on a collision basis that will equal the savaging blast of an exploding hydrogen bomb.

Could this be what the Soviets were testing a safe five hundred miles from their North Pacific bastions? Colonel Beardon believes they have been experimenting with "Star Wars" weapons systems that work precisely in this fashion and are capable of massive energy transformations. He stands firm on his conviction that this is a likely explanation for what happened in the Pacific that "dreadful night" of April 9, 1984. He has kept records of approximately fifty startling phenomena remarkably similar to that huge pulsating cloud soaring into the stratosphere. What would result from a Soviet scalar electromagnetic beam test, deduces the colonel, is an incredible "cold explosion," as close to instantaneous as you can get, snatching an enormous amount of energy from the spot where the beams converged—so much energy would pour inward to fill the emptiness that the collision of all that energy would produce the effects of a thermonuclear explosion, but without the blinding light and steel-hard shock waves associated with the blast of a hydrogen bomb.

In other words, instead of an explosion caused by the fission-fusion-fission release of energy at hundreds of millions of degrees, just the opposite happened—a *cold* explosion—the total extraction of all energy, happening so quickly that the result is an energy vacuum.

"Imagine such an explosion on the front lines of NATO," warned Colonel Beardon. "We'd have frozen soldiers within seconds."

It would be gratifying if we could offer the comforting words of a final explanation to that fantastic, mysterious, enormous cloud howling into the atmosphere in April 1984.

But we don't have the answer.

The geophysical scientists don't have the answer.

Meteorologists don't even want to talk about it, because according to everything they know about weather, that cloud was absolutely impossible.

It seems incredible that in our time, with all our weather and other satellites in Earth orbit, with a vast array of scientific equipment within the oceans, with global data collection of weather events, with superpowerful computers available to delve into every natural occurrence, no one has yet come up with an explanation of what that cloud was.

5

IT'S ALL IN THE PERCEPTION

Sightings of incredible events, of godly figures, of dazzling lights in the skies—moments that border on the miraculous to the individual involved—have always given us food for deep thought. Not everyone sees the same event in the same way, because vision differs, range of hearing varies from one person to another, emotional comfort levels change from hour to hour and day to day, and what we believe, what we know, is based on what we learned as youngsters, and that forms the path of perception and belief we follow for most of our lives.

Understanding of our physical world also varies greatly from one individual to another, and this affects enormously what we see, perceive, and derive from observation. The average person looking up at a cloudy sky judges that dark overcast usually means rain or snow. But the experienced meteorologist, pilot, or ship's captain sees far more from the same scene—the clouds indicate whether they bear rain, if they precede a frontal passage, how strongly the winds are blowing. In short, being able to "read" what we see precedes what we understand.

Because most of us are subjected to some sort of theological training from our earliest days, we grow into adulthood with rock-hard beliefs that there is a God, or that there definitely is not; that angels are real, or that they are simply twisted emotions; that Satan is a figure as real as any other, or that the devil is really a story used to frighten ill-behaved children.

What we perceive makes up our world. What follows

in this chapter contains stirring moments, events, and passages from people who are absolutely serious that what they encountered and what they believe was and is real. But it is not fair to the reader not to point out that past training and experience can distort one's perception of an event, and that there are not only two but often many sides to any story.

REALITY AND THE DISTORTION OF REALITY

The word *mirage* is often associated with hallucination. People see rivers where none exist, trees growing where there is only barren desert, lakes where there is bone-dry rock, even mountains that are not really there.

Mirages are *not* hallucinations; they are *mirror images*, and they exist as an almost everyday occurrence in nature. Every time you look in the mirror you see a mirage. And even the best trained observers, researchers, and scientists are often completely fooled by their perception of what they see—a reflection of some far-off place that seems to be absolutely real and very close to them.

Perhaps the single most dramatic case of a mirage fooling trained observers—in this case explorer-scientists with vast experience—involved such noted persons as Admiral Robert Peary, discoverer of the North Pole, and Roy Chapman Andrews and their accompanying party of explorers and hunters. This group in 1906 was searching for a new way to cross the American continent's northern reaches, seeking the long-sought Northwest Passage.

They knew that earlier expeditions had run into formidable obstacles looking for the same goal. In 1818, Sir James Ross and his party sailed into the waters of Lancaster Sound. This would be the opening move in the drive to chart the Northwest Passage for future commerce. They never went any farther. Before them loomed a tremendous cascade of high and jagged mountains. It was impossible to go on. After great expense, time, and energy, they returned in defeat to England.

Eighty-eight years later, in 1906, Admiral Peary, on

his way to chart the Northwest Passage, entered Lancaster Sound, confirmed the mountains first seen by Ross, and prepared to make charts of the mountains so that they (Peary and his team) might find a passage through the mountain range. Instead, Peary was assailed by ice floes that blocked further advances. He called the unexplored territory Crocker Land. Returning to the United States, he prepared a report on his findings, which was submitted to the American Museum of Natural History. After two attempts spanning nearly a century, the Northwest Passage remained blocked by the towering mountain range.

Then came the wonder of 1913 and a lesson in perception that stunned all concerned.

Donald MacMillan was regarded as one of the best Arctic explorers in the world. In 1913, seven years after Peary returned without success, the American Museum of Natural History funded and equipped MacMillan in another attempt to break through and chart a Northwest Passage—if one were possible through the treacherous mountains. He was also charged with exploring Crocker Land and preparing accurate charts and terrain maps of the area.

MacMillan's exploration was dogged with accidents and misfortunes that would have turned back lesser men. His confidence was hardly enhanced when he couldn't find the mountains that had blocked Ross and Peary. Finally, many miles west of where the earlier explorers had marked the maps on their charts, he saw the mountains come into view. But . . . how could they be so many miles away from where other experienced explorers had seen and charted them? Putting aside his questions until he could reach the mountain range, he was blocked—as Peary had been—by massive ice floes.

MacMillan made an immediate decision. He selected his most experienced and able explorers and the new team began crossing the treacherous ice floes. They maintained a steady progress under fearful conditions toward the mountains.

But the mountains began to move away from them. As fast as they closed the distance to the towering mountain range, the great peaks kept receding before them. The experience seemed absolutely impossible, yet this was precisely what was happening.

Because the mountains were never there in the first place! They were reflections of a mountain range unknown miles away. Sunlight reflecting from the ice and snow of the distant range bounced at an angle back into the sky and, striking inversion layers of air that functioned as mirrors, reflected the scene of the mountains down into Crocker Land and the shoreline bays.

The day came when the explorers had the mountains in view, still impossibly distant. As sunset dropped about them and the mirage reflection dissipated—the mountains became phantom images and then vanished completely.

Before MacMillan and his men was a vast expanse of ice as far as they could see. The only real obstacle to finding the Northwest Passage had never existed.

Sometimes an area of unusual energy can be *felt* but not seen. In most cases that's not at all mysterious. Microwaves, for example, in both home radar ranges and mighty tracking systems can burn right through objects in their path. Microwave energy, just like radio and television signals and electromagnetic radiation from power lines, is powerful, sometimes lethal, but remains invisible no matter how dangerous its effects.

There are also occasions when a form of energy, or an apparition (perhaps the same thing), or something unexplainable occupies the same area as people and is never observed by the human eye or other senses. However, objects invisible to us within the visible spectrum of light may show up in ultraviolet or infrared. And photographs taken of empty space or an open field can hold great surprises for the photographer, especially when the film is processed and printed and there on the photograph is *something* that the human eye never detected when the picture was shot.

John Craig of Winnipeg was unexpectedly thrust into a mystery that to this day defies explanation—a mystery that was never seen by the unaided human eye, but was captured on ordinary color film.

The photographer was a waitress in Winnipeg. No one recalls her name. What John Craig explained was that he did know the woman was a passenger on a commercial airliner flight. Returning from a trip that was either a vacation or visiting a distant family home, during which she had taken many pictures, she noticed she had one frame left of unexposed film in her camera. As the airliner passed through an area of building cumulus clouds, she placed the camera lens close to her window and snapped the shutter. All she could see before taking the picture was clouds and sky.

The year was 1982, and at that time John Craig frequented the restaurant where this waitress worked. During a conversation she described her airliner flight. But she had something special to add. "She told me," John Craig related, "that she had taken her last frame of film of sky and clouds, looking through her airliner window. She was amazed when the picture revealed, well, something she could hardly believe. She gave me a copy of the picture. I had already heard about the photo from other people who were greatly excited about it. I was pretty curious by the time I got to see the shot. When she gave me the photo, I kept staring at it. She told me again, emphasizing the point, that only clouds and sky were visible to her when she snapped the picture.

"But on that last frame, when it was printed, there was a great Jesus-like figure amidst the clouds! It was unmistakable. An incredible scene. We can't tell just how large this figure was, in terms of size, except that obviously it was much bigger than a man. Whatever that picture captured, it was both shocking and wonderful to everyone who saw the photo."

The photograph is grainy. It is anything but professional, yet there is no question the figure looms huge in the sky. Most people who held the photo and studied it intently believe that they are seeing something absolutely not of the world in which we live.

The original photograph was sent to Matt DiPalma of Graphics Militaire in Gainesville, Florida, an experienced artist and computer operator who specializes in detailed analysis of photographs. He subjects them to computer enhancement to bring out details not visible in the original photo. Computer enhancement is now an accepted process in military reconnaissance and deep-space photography and is accepted in crime investigations. There is no question that a figure, bearded, with a flowing robe and sandals looms amidst the clouds.

No one can explain the figure. Those who lean in the religious direction absolutely believe it is a Jesus-like figure. It may be, but there is no way to be certain. No one knows what Jesus *really* looked like. Painters through the ages who have depicted Christ have painted the faces of a man barely recognizable from one to the other.

But one thing is certain. What the human eye could not see, looming in the sky miles above the earth, *is there.*

It is not a natural phenomenon, it is not a cloud, it is not the distortion of lights and shadows. It is simply there—a great, unexplained mystery that, until another explanation comes forth, must be listed as supernatural.

A HELPING HAND

Elisabeth L. Barnes of Maryland is a woman of many talents—sharp, skilled, and capable. Among her favorite pastimes in life is flying. She is not a heroine of fabled flights, she holds no records, and her time airborne is on the low side of the scale. She describes herself as a pilot, "although very much a neophyte at 257 hours logged time. I have been flying off and on for twenty years, as my money held out. I am in awe of the 'old-timers' who have grown up with flying and have the local and world experience that I have not been able, so far, to obtain."

But one thing I do share with [other pilots] is a

supernatural experience that I had when I had just learned to solo. I was practicing touch-and-go takeoffs and landings at Lee Airport in Edgewater, Maryland, back in 1968. I was flying a single-engined Piper, a PA-22-108, a nice, very forgiving airplane. I suppose I had been given the usual lessons concerning stalls, where the nose of the aircraft is hauled back until it sticks up at about a 45-degree angle, and then the wing loses lift, and then there's only one place for the airplane to go—*down*.

On this day, I was making an approach to Runway 30, over a highway with telephone poles and wires below. The top of the nose of the plane was lined up on the horizon, as I had been taught, when suddenly the plane felt and sounded all wrong. I remember checking the engine sounds and gauges—no problems there. I probably felt the loss of lift and missed the sound of air over the wings during an incipient stall. But the thought of a stall never crossed my mind. Stalls were those things that took place with a very definite sharp break. The nose snaps down in a motion that can't be misjudged for anything else.

I believe I was at about two hundred feet above the ground. A stall at that height is suicidal. I remember feeling very helpless and out of control.

All of a sudden, I remember myself praying, "I don't want to die now, God, please, not now." I was really in trouble and I knew it. I had not been inside a church for years but somehow I knew Who would help me.

He did. Suddenly I felt a "total acceptance" that other pilots have talked about. I felt what I can only describe as a hand push me back into my seat. I let go of the yoke completely. I was not at all afraid. Of course, that's all that marvelous little trainer needed to get back on track. As soon as the nose went down I felt the lift back under the wings. I don't know how much altitude I lost but it was negligible because I was able to complete, somewhat shakily, my approach.

After landing, I called it a day, probably because shock had caught up with me. I remember thinking to myself, "Wow, I got out of that mess really well." I had totally forgotten, at that point, the prayer I had prayed and was thinking that my own "expertise" had rescued me. It wasn't until years later, when through some heartbreaking experiences I had reached the bottom of the barrel and had no place else to look but up, that the Lord Jesus Christ, now my Lord Jesus Christ, reminded me that he had taken care of me on that day.

Elisabeth Barnes became familiar with "miracle" stories of other pilots, men and women she had never met but had heard or read about, and was convinced of "the Lord's supernatural power reaching out to rescue them. I am convinced of that. My story is not as exciting perhaps compared to theirs, but it means everything to me.

"All I know is that my life is in the hands of my Lord. . . . Truth can be found in the strangest of places. . . . It takes courage to go look in places that other people avoid. But the rewards can be wonderful."

There's a critical postscript to what Elisabeth Barnes related of that moment when her airplane stalled just two hundred feet above the ground. She believes absolutely, she knows, that someone that wasn't her regained the lifting power of her plane's wings.

She had explained, "I let go of the yoke completely," and added that this was "all that marvelous little trainer needed to get back on track."

She is certainly right—aerodynamically—that she had help. When an airplane stalls in the manner that befell her, the pilot needs to do two things to avoid hitting the ground. One is to go to full power immediately. Elisabeth Barnes never mentioned shoving the throttle forward, so that was out.

When she "let go of the yoke completely" she was actually ensuring that she would crash: the only way to regain control at stall speed is for the pilot to shove the control yoke as far forward as it will go, and do so instantly, to get the nose down so the airplane speeds up and regains lift. She was too low for that maneuver to succeed.

There was no way that airplane could have recovered as she describes *unless* help came from beyond the laws of aerodynamics. Several pilots went up in a PA-22, the same model she was flying, to reenact the situation in which Barnes found herself, only they repeated the maneuver at a much higher altitude than two hundred feet!

In the stall, without adding power, and "letting go of the yoke completely," every time the maneuver was flown the airplane fell downward in the stall, and without the pilot shoving forward on the yoke, it always lost between five hundred and one thousand feet before it regained flying speed and control.

"Somebody else" saved that airplane, and Elisabeth Barnes with it.

A MOTHER'S DREAM

During World War II, First Lieutenant Herbert T. Kurz was the pilot of a four-engined B-24 Liberator bomber in the 98th in Bombardment Squadron (Heavy) of the 11th Bombardment Group, flying with the 98th in combat from May 12, 1943, to February 24, 1945. He was also the assistant intelligence officer of the 98th, and in sworn testimony affirmed that he had "personal, firsthand knowledge" of the events that follow—one of the most astonishing episodes of the entire war.

The detailed information that follows is provided through the kind permission of George E. Kurz of Chattanooga, Tennessee, the son of Lieutenant Herbert T. Kurz.

On January 20, 1944, one of the B-24s from the 98th

Squadron was lost to anti-aircraft fire during a strike against Wotje Atoll, part of the Marshall Islands in the Pacific Ocean. A determined search by the Air Force and the Navy, covering the entire area of the bombing mission and the routes to and from the target, failed to discover any survivors, bodies, or even wreckage of the heavy bomber.

Soon afterward the squadron moved its operations base to Kwajalein Atoll. They were barely settled in when the squadron commander, Major Allen H. Wood, "informally called together several officers, including myself," Herbert Kurz said in his testimony, "and read a letter to us that had come from the mother of one of the enlisted men that had been aboard Hopkins's plane. I remember that the man had been from New England. She described a dream that she had, that the plane her son was on had gone down, but that he was alive on an island called 'Lae,' which she dreamed was in our area of operations.

"Major Woods was puzzled by the letter, and wanted some suggestions and ideas about what to do. We checked the maps we had available but couldn't find any 'Lae' in our area. . . ."

The pilots looked at one another; several shrugged. There wasn't much to say. In fact, these guys were in a life-and-death situation with the Japanese and the latter were doing the best they could to kill the Americans in their heavy bombers.

Now they were supposed to search for an island described by the mother of a missing airman—because the mother had had a dream. The whole idea seemed preposterous.

A mother's *dream* . . .? Were they supposed to fly into Japanese-defended territory on the basis of some extrasensory perception about the possible fate of her missing son? And they'd never heard of the alleged island of Lae, it wasn't on their maps (and their best maps were from *National Geographic*), and the search would have to be carried out in bombers without fighter escort.

The concept seemed crazy.

There was another burr in the situation. Frank Washburn was the bombardier on the same airplane as the missing airman who was dreamt about by his mother. Washburn was immensely popular with his squadron, and the squadron strongly wanted to confirm whether Washburn was alive or dead on any one of several islands where his plane might have gone down.

Arthur K. "Dutch" Herold, intelligence officer, added an enigmatic twist to the bizarre story:

> One thing you have to know about Frank Washburn—he was no ordinary man. . . . the circumstances surrounding the loss of his plane, his disappearance, and his ultimate fate were far more mysterious and puzzling than [any] other air casualties. His grave was verified by comrades in one location and seen by a neighbor in another place about one-eighth the length of the equator from the first. *Neither grave has yet produced a body.* . . .
>
> If Frank was out of the ordinary, some of the circumstances surrounding his disappearance border on the extraordinary, if not downright mysterious. Some of the people involved in those circumstances with him died at the scene. Some others have died since. . . .

The B-24 carrying Washburn set up its target run and Herold added, the pilot "turned over control of the plane and its forty 100-pound bombs to Frank at 2:24 A.M. From that point, the destiny of Frank Washburn would have slipped from our view forever, except for some peculiar twists of fate. . . ."

> Major Wood also revealed an incredible story contained in a letter to him as Commanding Officer. The mother of Staff Sergeant Allen Hibbert, one

of the enlisted men . . . wrote that she'd seen her son in a dream. His plane had crashed, but her son was alive and on an island called "Lae."

"None of the maps we have in the squadron show an island with such a name," Woody said, "and I want your advice as to what course of action we should take."

The entire group volunteered to fly an unofficial "search" but the first order of business was to search maps that might show an island called "Lae." The belief was strong among the pilots (a naturally superstitious group of humans anyway) that such an island must exist since it was so vivid in a dream from the mother of a missing crew member.

An intelligence officer, Lieutenant John Gartland, did some intensive searching and came up a winner. There *was* such an island, in the Marshall's Group—but it was about 260 miles west of Wotje Atoll where the missing B-24 had made its bomb run. The Navy had been contacted before about Lae Island, but replied that after earlier requests they had identified the island but that there was "nothing" on that small atoll. That was still more than enough for the bomb group.

"On June 10, 1944," Dutch Herold's account continues, "two pilots made history. Lieutenants Leland A. Bates and Arthur H. Peterson, attached to the 98th Squadron from the 42nd Squadron, performed what is believed to be the only photographic mission on record flown over an area not considered a target, and which was mounted solely on the basis of a mother's dream."

From Kwajalein, the new base for the B-24 bombers, the two B-24 pilots soon found the tiny atoll of Lae. But, "What else they found was beyond belief. Photos were taken which verified the existence of a manmade lean-to structure of palm leaves in a clearing. *It was never re-*

ported before on any landings by the Navy. . . ."

The next turn in the story is quite astonishing if not cruel. The 98th Squadron got word that this later Navy search verified the existence of the clearing and the lean-to and also found a recently dug shallow grave. Evidently, the search planes couldn't distinguish the grave either by sighting or on camera. The grave had a crude wooden marker in the shape of a cross over one end of it. The name scratched onto the cross was also crudely done, but clearly visible. The name appearing on the marker was "F. WASHBURN." The Navy reconfirmed its earlier findings—no humans *living* on the island. . . .

Kurz wondered if there were no humans on the island, what happened to those who'd buried "F. WASHBURN" or made the cross? Of course, we don't know if ever there was a body in the grave. It seems odd that no evidence exists that the body was exhumed for identification. . . .

Ordinarily, the incidents reported here would have no more said or known about them. They would be assigned to that nebulous category or classification permitting human life and tremendous amounts of equipment to be assigned to oblivion with the stroke of a pen. The most glaring self-declarations of both sloppy and deliberate mismanagement during World War II were the phrases "lost in combat" or "lost (or damaged) due to enemy action." Even where human life was concerned, no greater effort was made to save or recover it, in many instances, than the effort required to save or recover a lost ammunition belt or a mess kit spoon.

There are many indicators that such lack of effort to recover Frank Washburn existed, although the "unofficial" search that was authorized based on the dream of a mother seems to indicate that a greater effort was expended in this case. . . .

There remains a mystery surrounding the grave on Lae Atoll, but no one knows to this day if the grave contained the body of Washburn or that of someone else. And it may well have been Hibbert and other crew members, still alive on Lae Atoll, who buried Washburn.

A final note from George E. Kurz, written in 1987:

By a miserable stroke of fate, Sexy Sue IV was hit by the "meager and inaccurate" anti-aircraft fire (reported by other crews), from the ship in Wotje Lagoon. . . . Regardless of the reason, the plane crashed on the island, or possibly in shallow water [at] nearby Wotje. It did not explode or burn immediately on impact, and most of the crew survived the crash. . . . Sgt. Estes and possibly another crewman died as a result of the crash or were killed by the Japanese and buried on Wotje. The remaining crewmen were taken to Kwajalein for POW classification and interrogation. . . . None of the crewmen were listed by the Japanese as POWs, however.

Some POW camp survivors, captured earlier, reported being taken west by way of Eniwetok Atoll. Natives on Lae reported that their island also had been used by the Japanese as a stopover on the way to Eniwetok. However, an assault on Eniwetok was begun on 17 February 1944 by the 22nd Marines. I believe that Frank was among the crash survivors being evacuated by that same route, but that the evacuation was disrupted due to the increase of U.S. combat pressure in that area. I believe that he died from wounds or illness and was buried on an island of Lae Atoll by other POWs in that group.

I believe that the mother of one of the crew-men had a dream about her son when he was with Frank, and that she identified Lae Atoll in a way that utterly defies explanation.

Finally, I believe that the remains of Frank Washburn, his service honorable and his story told, lie in peace on an island of Lae Atoll in the Marshall Islands.

A mother's dream. What do we call it? ESP? Telepathy connecting her to her son halfway around the world and pinpointing a tiny island her son's bomber group did not even know existed, but about which her dream and her letter to the 11th Bombardment Group was uncannily accurate?

Whatever it was, it was real. *It happened.* A mission in war was mounted solely on the basis of that dream.

"THE MAN UPSTAIRS"

Gordon Codding, from Kingman, Arizona, was one of those pilots from World War II who joined the Air Force, went through cadet school and flight training, and then watched that war wind down before they had the chance to try their new wings in combat. He graduated Flight Class 44B, and the powers that be, watching the Japanese collapsing on every front, moved Codding and many of his fellow pilots directly into the Air Transport and Ferrying Command. Codding was to discover that, while he didn't get into any combat engagements, he would experience two events stranger than anything he ever believed would happen to him.

The first of these moments involved five other pilots as well; otherwise, Codding told his friends, "I doubt if I would have believed, myself, what happened." One of their first assignments sent the six men to an old training field in the deep South to pick up a bunch of Stearman PT-13 and PT-17 single-engined biplane primary trainers. Codding called it an "old training field" because it had already been deactivated, and the planes would soon be falling apart unless they were flown to proper care and packaging in an army field outside Salt Lake City, Utah.

The Stearmans fly *slowly*. With a stiff head wind, the pilots could watch cars passing them on the highways below.

But it was more than head winds that made their long cross-country flight take much longer than anyone had planned. "The flight went well as we slowly flew west," Codding explained. "Slowly, because we had made unexpected friends with six 'traveling saleswomen' who drove about the country selling cosmetics. It was a nifty arrangement. We all stayed in the same motels at night, they'd drive us out to the local airfield in the morning, wave to us as we took off and headed out for our next stop, and then the ladies would get in their cars and floor their gas pedals. We watched them pass beneath us and at our next airport stop, there they'd be, waiting for us. That was such slow flying I could have made better speed and time in an ancient 1929 Lincoln-Page I used to fly in Carlsbad, New Mexico. But it was a terrific trip."

All good things must come to an end, and the day arrived when the six pilots prepared for their final leg into Salt Lake City. The pilots began to pay special attention to the condition of the engines and airplanes. It had been fun and games up until now, but ahead of them were some dangerous mountains. Because these airplanes lacked the power to fly over those mountains, they would have to "wind and find" their way through low canyons. Under any conditions, flying this way can be "begging for trouble."

"We inspected the airplanes the best we could, and then we got smart," Codding recalled.

> With our own money, because the Air Force wouldn't pay for this kind of service, we hired a local aircraft mechanic to go over our ships for us. He did, and whatever he found wrong or needing

attention he fixed and tweaked. He gave us all a long look and asked if we'd flown anything like the Stearmans through mountain canyons. He warned us that our airplanes had been battered pretty well through years of service as trainers by pilots still learning the game, and the engines no longer could put out their advertised power. We paid him special attention about what problems we might expect, and the best way to fly through the canyon bottoms. It was great advice, but the problem was we were neophytes at mountain flying and we couldn't tell one canyon from another.

So we gathered our maps, each of us with one flight chart and one automotive map—which had more detail in the mountain passes and canyons than what they gave us for aerial navigation—and we fired up and took off for the last leg to the west. The weather favored us, the sky mostly clear and the afternoon sun painting a golden glow in the western sky before us.

That's when we learned our first lesson as to how really dumb we were. You just do *not* try to fly through mountain passes or canyons, if you're flying west, in the late afternoon, because it turned that golden glow into an eye-watering, nearly blinding glare as the lowering sun smacked us right in the eyes. We were trying like crazy to find the *right* canyon to enter and we could hardly see. This was no joke. If you pick the *wrong* canyon you're begging to become a statistic, because you don't have enough room to turn around if you fly into a dead-end canyon, and that means a guaranteed crash. Especially in the bunch of training wearies in which we were flying.

We began flying north and south, like dogs running with their tails tucked low, trying anxiously, nearly desperately, to find the canyon entrance that matched the description given us by the mechanic. Hope was running out faster than our burning off fuel.

Suddenly we spotted a bright, an almost brilliant, yellow Piper Cub circling far out in front of us and much closer to the ground than we were. The Cub was circling right along our possible route. It was strange and it became stranger, for it seemed the Cub was circling until all six of us caught sight of that airplane and turned toward it. The moment it was obvious we were flying after the Cub it banked out of its circling turn and flew directly into a canyon.

That did it for us. We *knew* we were intended to follow the Cub. We also assumed—using hand signals to one another—that if that Cub, with a lot less power than we had, could squeeze through that canyon, then the rest of us could follow him all the way by flying Indian File, one after the other, with myself in the Number Six position.

That "strange" feeling? It became stronger, for the Cub flew just as fast as we did, not faster, not slower, but at our *exact* speed. And even stranger was the fact that we were always able to keep the Cub clearly in sight. Although the sun was on the other side of the Cub, it seemed to be as brightly illuminated on those parts of the airplane that should have been in shadow. It didn't seem "right," but we sure weren't going to try to figure it out then, for we were now seven airplanes winding their way between steep mountain walls.

Well, we flew through that canyon and it was incredible as we emerged on the other side of the mountains—because we were lined up perfectly with our destination airfield, via the Mormon

Temple as a sighting landmark. Surprise! That Cub, if it *was* a Cub, *vanished* as soon as the lead PT-17 emerged from the canyon, the rest of us following right behind.

On the ground we gathered to try to understand what had happened. No one on the airfield knew a thing about the Cub. They had seen *six*, not seven airplanes, emerging from the canyon, and all they saw were our six biplanes.

I decided right then and there that to pass this off just because it didn't "fit" was a stupid thing to do. As far as I was concerned, and none of the other pilots had cause to argue the point, we had been helped by "The Man Upstairs" who sent us a guide in our serious "moment of need," and nothing will ever change my mind, and it never has.

This episode wasn't the only out-of-the-ordinary event that took place on Gordon Codding's cross-country trip.

On this same ferry flight I got into a problem while we were flying somewhere over Missouri. Being Tail-End Charley in the Number Six position meant I could fall out from our Indian File formation and my absence could easily be overlooked for a time.

I lost the engine oil cap over Missouri, and when you run out of oil you're going straight for engine seizure and a possible fire. As I saw the oil siphoning out and the telltale dark streaks I started looking for a suitable landing spot. I knew I could always do the old "barnstormer's trick" by slipping into a farmer's pasture, but a real landing strip would be much better.

At just about the time I expected that engine to quit cold from lack of oil, I caught sight of what I'd call a traditional, old-fashioned, grass-

roots flying field. It was right out of a flying
story: an old windmill set up next to the office
shack, an old gas truck with a paint-peeling
pump, a beat-up prewar pickup truck, all on the
edge of an open field so you could always have
room to take off or land directly into the wind.
The whole place had that haunting familiar look
I'd read in so many flying stories as a youngster
back in the thirties.

I brought the Stearman down into the wind
and landed, taxiing quickly to the shack that
served as an office, alongside the battered old
hangar. As I cut the switches and the propeller
ground to a halt, an old gentleman—just like he
also came out of one of those old flying tales—
came out of the shack. He looked up at me and
grinned.

"Looks like you might be needing a little oil,"
he said in what I guessed was a Missouri twang.
What an understatement! The spray from the oil
tank had blackened the fuselage all the way back
to the tail.

He said he "just happened" to have enough
oil of the right type and "figured" he might also
"just happen to have" something to plug the filler
pipe. So he rummaged around in an ancient tool-
box on his truck and came out with a "gas tank
cap" that "just by accident" was an *exact* fit for
my oil tank. Very gratefully I paid him for the oil,
the cap, some fuel, his labor, thanked him a dozen
times for his help, started up the engine, and was
on my way to rejoin the other five planes.

Later, I inquired about that old grassroots
field after I landed. The local people where we'd
stopped for the night looked at me like I was
crazy. The local airport operator, and the pilots
who regularly flew in that part of the country,
said there wasn't any such airfield where I'd been.

They even brought out a bunch of maps and charts and retraced my route. They knew every airfield and operator for more than a hundred miles in every direction. A lot of them flew the same route regularly that I'd been on, and they repeated there wasn't any such airfield there. Neither had anyone ever met, or even heard of, any person to match my description of that marvelous old gentleman I'd met who helped me.

Someone else had provided help, and everything I needed, at an airfield that didn't exist, by a man who didn't exist either. Not in this world, anyway. Then, after the episode with that Cub leading us through the mountain canyon, there couldn't *ever* be any doubt.

The Man Upstairs.

He'd been there for me both times.

HOW HIGH IS HEAVEN?

I am grateful to a French news correspondent who, at his insistence, must remain unnamed in these pages, as he explains, "to protect his sources and keep open his lines of communication."

He explained further that were it not for what he judges as the "absolute reliability" of his source, from within the former Soviet Union, he would never have passed on the information that follows "because then I would be considered as crazy as my source."

In June 1985 those in the control center for the Soviet space station *Salyut 7* were stunned by the voices of the cosmonauts reporting a sight so bizarre that they began to doubt their own senses. High overhead, orbiting Earth, the cosmonauts of *Salyut 7* were in the 155th day of their mission.

The three cosmonauts were at their duty stations when "suddenly a dazzling orange light enveloped the *Salyut*." Commander Atkov and cosmonauts Soloviev and

Kizim reported that the light was so blinding that at first they thought there had been an explosion or a fire in some part of the station. With strained voices they added that all three men "for several minutes seem to have been struck blind."

When their vision returned they looked through the portholes of the *Salyut*—and were struck dumb.

"We are seeing faces," they told their ground control.

They were ordered to repeat, slowly, what they had said. Atkov slowly and deliberately explained what they could see.

"Outside the ship . . . we are able to see seven faces. They . . . there are seven, they are huge, human bodies with wings. They look like what we call on Earth angels."

The seven "faces" kept pace with the *Salyut 7* orbiting the Earth at nearly *five miles a second* for a period of ten minutes, and then, abruptly, they vanished.

In the excited exchange between ground control and *Salyut 7*, the cosmonauts added that perhaps they had all gone crazy at the same time. After several more days passed, they were more convinced than ever that they had all suffered some kind of inexplicable "group hallucination."

Twelve days later, on the 167th mission day, the three men were joined by three additional cosmonauts who reached the station aboard the *Soyuz T-12* spacecraft—Volk, Dzhanibovek, and Savistkaya. Now there were five men and one woman aboard the station.

The station was again enveloped in the dazzling orange light, and now six cosmonauts found themselves temporarily blinded by the glare. Once again ground control was as stunned as the cosmonauts in space, who radioed, "We can see the faces of seven angels . . . smiling. They are smiling like they share a glorious secret with us. Each angel is huge, like the first time. They are each as big as an airliner! They stayed with us a couple of minutes, and then . . . they are gone. We cannot see them anymore."

These exchanges between *Salyut 7* and ground control

were kept under the strictest secrecy. The extraordinary event was never known outside until a top engineer from the Soviet manned space program left his homeland and came to the United States.

Any and all discussion on the subject seemed to have been forbidden. All questions referring to the incident went without response.

The French correspondent found it incredible "that nobody even seems to try to obtain more information on this remarkable, even incredible, event. And I wish to emphasize as strongly as I can that it is not myself who is telling you what happened. It is the Soviet military crew who said that they saw the 'angels.' "

6
WHO CARES IF IT'S NOT REAL?
IT WORKS!

Is dowsing supposed to be supernatural? If you accept the scientific explanation that dowsing is not a normal human ability, and you believe dowsing—that is, finding underground water, for example, by the movements of a forked stick or angled wires—is real, then you have accepted that the supernatural occurs within the abilities of many thousands of people. In short, you're a believer in the supernatural.

However, if you feel that dowsing is a normal electrical or magnetic function of the human body, then dowsing becomes just one more natural ability.

In specific terms, dowsers hunt for water, metal, jewelry, plumbing, tunnels, or other objects deep within the ground. The dowser (or water witch, as many are still called) holds a forked twig of birch or hazelwood (the favorite), or even a twisted coat hanger. In more modern times, dowsing (or divining) rods have been manufactured to specific technical configurations and mass produced for the U.S. Department of Defense. The individual walks slowly across a field (searching for an underground well or river, for example), and when directly over the water below, the wood, metal, or other material will move with startling force. Two rods may cross by turning inward, or the forked twig may snap down suddenly or perform some other movement that leaves no question that the water will be found below.

It is strange that, despite the many thousands of authenticated cases, most scientists continue to ridicule the entire concept of dowsing. The dowsers, fortunately, go right on finding water, often in places where the most modern scientific equipment has failed to detect so much as a smidgen of moisture.

One issue, of course, is determining why dowsing works at all. Another is finding out why dowsing works for some people but not for others. (And it works, sometimes phenomenally, the first time for people who have never seen dowsing or tried it themselves.)

In past centuries mostly men were dowsers (and still are, for some unexplained reason), perhaps because men did most of the traveling. They used their talents to find water when it was needed desperately and there was no other hope of alleviating a drought, or simply because more water was needed for increasing populations, irrigation, or some other reason.

Superstition in olden times was a way of life; the dangers of the spirit world were found on all sides. Dowsers (also known as diviners, from a "divine touch") were judged to be blessed in some magical or spiritual way, and the magic was judged as either good or bad according to each particular situation. At the time of the Inquisition, dowsers were classed as witches and were usually burned alive at the stake. It is little wonder that dowsing was often judged to be one of the black arts.

At least modern reactions to superstition has softened to social stigma rather than the rack or the flames, but there is still as much mystery today as in years gone past as to how and why dowsing works. There is obviously *something* in the physical and mental makeup of some people that grants them success in dowsing. Perhaps it is some match or link, a common magnetic frequency between their bodies and the substance they seek; when the two match, the twig or rod acts like a compass drawn to a powerful magnetic source. We have long known that the human brain transmits a radio signal in the 20–30 hertz band, and so does the planet we live on. Brain and planet both are electrical dynamos, no matter how different the strength of the signal. It is worth considering the effect when the frequency of the brain and planet signals match. Does the dowser respond to variations in these radio waves? The 20-hertz signal is as real as the signals transmitted by a radio antenna. Finding out how the various waves affect one another may clarify the reactions and even enable us to enhance the effect. Some neurological researchers are considering the idea that this matching of radio waves, on an extremely specific frequency, might even address the mysteries of telepathic messages.

Let us then accept that dowsing is real. It works, no matter what its detractors claim. At the same time, we know that the physical laws of the universe demand that you cannot get something for nothing. Everything is an exchange of energy in one form or another. The law *always* applies. Everything balances. Matter and energy can only be exchanged; neither is ever destroyed.

Consider another remarkable fact that was confirmed after extensive research by geobiologist Joseph Kirschvink of the California Institute of Technology: magnetite crystals are embedded in the tissue of the human brain. In an article accepted by the *Proceedings of the National Academy of Sciences*, Kirschvink reported that magnetite crystals of microscopic size have been discovered through new research tools for neuronic studies of the brain. Magnetite is among the hardest metals known, and while magnetite crystals are found in a huge variety of animals, ranging from bees to the blue whale, not until Kirschvink's work had the existence of these crystals been confirmed in human brain tissue.

The magnetite crystals in animals serve as a navigational system that responds to the magnetic fields of the earth. They function as a "built-in compass." Magnetite enables the animals to orient themselves along magnetic field lines of the planet and use these lines as "magnetic highways" to travel with startling accuracy, from the short distances insects travel to fish and birds who migrate each year over thousands of miles.

There is as yet no confirmation that magnetite in certain humans is the source for their ability to use divining rods to locate water or metals underground. Current research is concentrating on why *spin echoes*, which appear as "odd blips," are found when researchers carry out magnetic resonance images of the human brain.

The jury is still out on the final answer, but there is an enormous record of more than circumstantial evidence. What frustrates scientists are those times when the scientists have plumbed fields with their elaborate devices and found nothing, and then the dowsing rods twitch, point, or bend, and when people dig they find water directly below—specifically where scientists have just stated flatly there is no water to be found.

No one knows for certain when ancient cultures, from the earliest farmers to nomads and hunters, came to understand that in times of great drought or other emergencies, when water supplies were needed desperately, there was a "miraculous" method of finding water where none could be seen. Historians have confirmed through ancient records that dowsing flourished more than seven thousand years ago. In those times the "gifted," as people knew them, were judged to be performing miracles in saving entire tribes when the rains stopped and bodies of water turned to sunbaked clay.

Carved into Egyptian columns, temples, and works of art are images of dowsers holding the very same type of forked sticks that modern "water witches" employ. In an ancient twist we cannot yet understand, these bas-relief pictures show the diviners of long-ago Egypt wearing strange headgear with what seems to be antennae jutting up and forward.

Archaeologists and historians have confirmed that the practice of searching for water with "special people" using wooden sticks or twigs was employed throughout almost all the known ancient world. The records, especially the pictorial finds carved into stone, show dowsers at work in cultures long gone, such as the Greeks, Medes, Persians, and Scythians.

In certain countries the dowsers were selected from the highest royalty, rulers believed to have special powers bestowed upon them by their gods. Chinese records show King Yu, from 4,200 years ago, carrying a dowsing rod while the everpresent faithful followed his every move with worshipping eyes.

The first known *written* references to dowsing are more than 450 years old. The oldest reference is the *De Re Metallica*, written by G. Agricola, which came off the press in the year 1546. Shortly afterward, *Cosmography* was completed by Sebastian Munster; both works were avidly sought after, because they described the practice of using forked sticks to find not only concealed water, but great lodes of precious metals as well.

The oldest European records indicate that dowsing for metals was an accepted industrial practice in the 1400s. German engineers and prospectors walked the steep slopes of the Harz Mountains in search of metallic ores. There was no need to look for water; it was plentiful enough. But fortunes could be made by finding veins of copper or iron or other metals. So successful were the Germans that when reports of their success reached England, Queen Elizabeth ordered her merchants to bring directly from Germany the same forked sticks the mountaineers were using so that they could be employed to seek out fresh ore veins in Britain's Cornish mines. After much of this mining finally faltered after the mines were stripped clean, water for industrial use and irrigation had become a major need, and the dowsers simply started out in new directions to find underground rivers and other water sources that could be tapped for wells.

No one was better known in the new industrial world than the sixteenth century's Greg Bauer, who was feted in his native land of Germany for an impressive string of accomplishments. Bauer, who gained renown throughout all Europe for his feats as a dowser, stood apart from the "water witches" due to the fact that he was an engineer and a scientist. He was judged one of the finest metallurgists in the world, achieved no small fame as a physicist, and astounded his contemporary mining engineers by teaching them how to seek out the lead, tin, and copper deposits of the Harz Mountains. He wrote reports of dowsers confounding the scientists of his time as the former wandered about valleys and mountains to discover ore veins where the latest scientific equipment failed to reveal anything of value beneath the surface.

"All alike," Bauer explained, "grasp the forks of the twigs with their hands, clenching their fists, it being necessary that the clenched fingers should be held towards the sky in order that the twig should be raised at that end where the two branches meet. Then they wander at random through the mountainous regions. It is said that the moment they place their feet on a vein the twig immediately turns and twists, and so by its action discloses the vein; when they move their feet again and go away from that spot the twig once more becomes immobile."

No one had any real clue to how such dowsing worked. Everything from radiations pouring forth from the ground and matching the radiated patterns of the dowsers to magic and sorcery was offered up by way of explanation. No one, however, *knew*, and the contentious arguments were put aside in favor of continued success. And modern events, some 400 years later, fit the same pattern.

The year was 1952, with World War II having ended barely seven years before, and war raging anew, this time in Korea and the Middle East. British forces were growing in strength in Germany during their postwar occupation. A new base had been selected for an expanded British military force, but army engineers approached Colonel Harry Grattan with the somber news that if the campsite were to be built as planned, they would suffer a critical shortage of water as soon as troops occupied their new quarters. Water could be piped or trucked in, but its expense and major effort would be so excessive as to be unacceptable.

To the astonishment of his engineering teams, Colonel Grattan told his men that *he* would find them the water they needed. Their own searches for water, using the most modern engineering and scientific equipment in the world, hadn't turned up so much as a hint of water in the area of the new camp.

Grattan went into the woods, cut himself several forked hazel branches, and started off through the local countryside. His baffled engineers followed him and were startled to see the hazel twig suddenly snap downward so quickly it almost tore free from the colonel's hands.

"Dig here, gentlemen," Grattan told his engineers. Shaking their heads, they dug—straight down into a fabulous aquifer that from then on and for decades produced more than a million gallons of fresh water every day!

Colonel Grattan was more than a top British army engineer—he was also an avid student of unusual events in the history of the British Army. He had often made reference to the near-miracle of the fighting in World War I's Gallipoli military expedition.

During intense fighting under conditions of searing heat and dust, British troops poured ashore on the Gallipoli peninsula, and soon were faltering badly in the brutal temperature. Perspiring under the weight of their equipment and needing to forge ahead, the troops were on the edge of exhausting their physical strength. They were on the brink of being overrun by the enemy and slaughtered like helpless sheep. Not only had they used up all their water supply, but the Gallipoli peninsula was well known to be barren of any water above or below ground. Defeat seemed impossible to avoid.

A British trooper named Sapper Kelly moved out from his position. "I'll find water," he told his commanding officer, who thought him quite mad but elected to let Kelly perform whatever crazy notion he had in mind. The troops stared in disbelief as Kelly removed copper wire from their supply team, bent the copper into a divining rod, and started walking. Men beset with heat exhaustion, cracked lips, and burned skin followed Kelly with glazed eyes. Suddenly the copper rod snapped to one side. Kelly turned and shouted for every man who could use a shovel to dig down immediately.

One hundred yards from Divisional Headquarters, the top officers stared at the sudden fury of digging, and then heard jubilant shouts. Kelly had unerringly pointed the way to a deep underground spring with fresh, cold water. Water poured up at the rate of two thousand gallons every hour—in a land where even the natives swore that none existed and none had ever been found.

Top officers went to Kelly. There were a hundred thousand British troops at Gallipoli. Was there a chance he might find even more water? Every one of those hundred thousand men would require a gallon of water daily simply to stay alive. Was it even remotely possible to find a source that would produce one hundred thousand gallons of water *every day?*

Seven days later, the incredible Sapper Kelly had located another thirty-two wells—producing well in excess of the one hundred thousand gallons needed. This one dowser did what science said was impossible—and gave the British army the means to continue its battle campaign at Gallipoli.

It doesn't require a war to cause terrible widespread suffering and loss of life. Through the centuries, tens of millions of people have died when great droughts devastated their lands. This was the situation in 1925 in India. In this land of immense population, the rains on which so many millions counted to grow their crops had failed to appear. Agricultural land dried up and turned to dust. The British government, aided by other nations, made a huge effort to ease the suffering, but the task overwhelmed their resources. The thickly populated districts of Sholapur, Ahmednagar, and Bijapur were scenes of especially cruel suffering. Not only had the rains failed to come, but the wells that people depended upon simply to stay alive were critically low and threatened to fail completely. Frantically, local authorities set thousands of people to digging new wells so the population could at least survive. Hundreds of wells were gouged from the earth, but produced only dusty soil. One of the greatest natural disasters of all time was in the making.

Leaders of the Bombay Legislative Council gathered in emergency session to seek out a solution. They were already using every merchant ship and tanker available to ship in water, but it barely touched the needs of a population already counting its first casualties. Trains also were carrying in water, but this supply was also inadequate. And there was no way to build canals or viaducts in time to avert disaster.

The *only* hope left was to intensify the digging of wells. Indian engineers reported to the Council members that they had used every engineering system and device known, and that the situation was hopeless.

Almost. One man rose to his feet in the stormy meeting. "We have not tried everything. I say we use the services of Major C. A. Pogson to find water for us." The suggestion brought cries of dismay and jeering. Pogson was a so-called water witch, a diviner, and the engineers believed that such people were fakes, con artists, and worse—this Pogson fellow was simply another false hope.

But there was no alternative. Against protests that retaining him would make the Council members and engineers look ridiculous, the Council went through the political motions to hire Major Pogson. He was likely the first person ever to be hired as an official water witch and was given the impressive title of Official Water Diviner to the Government of Bombay.

The derision grew louder as Pogson began walking the countryside of the drought-stricken areas with divining rods in his hands. Every now and then, before the eyes of incredulous witnesses, the wooden twigs would rotate downward and Pogson would stop and point before his feet, telling the engineers to dig.

An article in the official *Indian Journal of Engineering* came directly to the point. "Out of 49 wells which have been sunk upon spots indicated by Major Pogson, only two have failed to produce water. It is a notable achievement." The article made it clear that Pogson's uncanny skill in locating water had certainly saved the lives of millions of people. The *Journal* continued: "It is a somewhat bitter pill to engineers to be told by an evening contemporary that a major is better than machines, yet there is more than a mickle of justification for this clever newspaper head. . . . Major Pogson can find water, it appears, when the machines specially designed for the purpose have failed. It is an interesting situation."

Once the Indian government had thrown away the barriers to *officially* hiring a diviner, the way was opened for other governments to follow. British Columbia soon had a dowser under employ. During World War II the island of Ceylon followed suit, and the Italian army storming into Ethiopia carried with it an "official staff" of water dowsers. Other governments and armies, not bothering with what they considered "official palaver," made it a new habit to have dowsers with them in areas where scarce water supplies promised to be a problem.

But it didn't require a war or a devastating national drought to bring an *official* dowser to the United States, and the event took place not in the early half of this century but as late as 1963. Dowsing was an old art well known in this country, part of the history and culture brought in with European immigrants. In the frontier, Indian, and farming territories, it was especially valuable to the settlers, but in general it was regarded as a quaint European custom or had something vaguely to do with religious rites. In short, dowsing was better left to the witches, cults, and other lesser members of the burgeoning

American society until it was actually needed. Then it assumed legitimacy and acceptance with almost a roar of approval.

Swampscott, Massachusetts, was such a place. The small town nestled within the curving northeastern coastline had for years been hustling desperately to find a "lost" underground source of water.

The search began in the mid-1940s and centered about the impressive mansion of Professor Elihu Thomson, one of the best-known and highly respected electrical engineering scientists in the world. Thomson had cofounded the General Electric Company, and his own inventions with electrical systems were both famous and in wide use worldwide. During the time he occupied the mansion, Thomson needed an independent supply of water for his experiments, especially those with advanced types of batteries.

But by 1944 the town elders had bought the property and turned it into Swampscott's community administrative offices. Surrounding the mansion, now town headquarters, were sweeping lawns of lush grass. Thomson had used his own water supply to keep his lawns and elaborate landscaping luxuriant and fresh.

The problem was that Swampscott, only fifteen miles north of Boston, lacked sufficient water to attend to the town *and* the lawns. With water in short supply, officials couldn't draw water from the regular town supply and watched in dismay as the estate lawns turned from lush green to brittle brown.

The Department of Public Works spent twenty years searching for the elusive underground water source Thomson had used. For two decades workers dug channels, ditches, wells, and all manner of holes in the estate trying to find the original water source. They called in mining experts and military crews, using mine detectors and anything that might locate water.

Swampscott's Folly soon became a joke to the citizenry, who watched their town funds disappearing into nonstop years of digging and cratering. At long last the town council admitted defeat. The water could not be found.

At a meeting in 1962, one brave soul asked why they hadn't tried a water dowser. Council members were aghast at the suggestion. Water dowsing smacked of witchcraft, and New England had a nasty history of burning witches alive. After the meeting Paul Polisson, who ran the town's public works, took it upon himself to read what was regarded as the final word on dowsing, *Henry Gross and his Dowsing Rod*, written by Kenneth Roberts.

Polisson's own reticence kept him from seriously considering the idea of water dowsing for Swampscott until he discovered that Roberts had done a lot more than just write a book about it. Roberts had sat in his studio in Maine, scanning a map of the island of Bermuda— an island that had no natural supply of fresh water—and then told officials on that island exactly where to start digging wells. He selected the only places on Bermuda where water actually did exist. His long-distance dowsing was successful.

That was enough for Polisson. In June 1963, Polisson gathered his work crews. They cut branches in the exact shape and size Roberts described in his book, slicing off the branches from willow, wild apple, and maple trees. Then, perhaps as a touch of protection against hoots and jeers if he alone was the guiding force behind the dowsing and it failed, he brought in top officials from other divisions of the town council.

The crew spread out in their search, dowsing rods extended before them. Sudden shouts brought everyone running to an elderly worker, Dutchy Emery. They watched in amazement as Emery stood stock still while the forked branch he gripped tightly rotated downward. "Hang on!" one shouted. "Grip it tighter!" another called. "Stay with it, Dutchy!" came a final yell.

Emery tried his best. The branch turned downward with such force it was scraping away the skin of Emery's

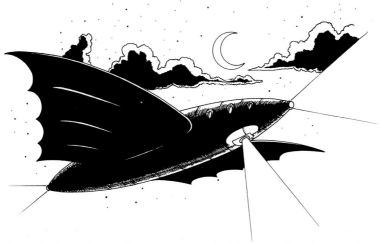

A rendering of one of the mystery airships seen by thousands of people in the western United States in 1896–97. The wings and brilliant searchlights have never been explained.

Art by Matt DiPalma

If ancient Chinese legends are true, then hundreds of years ago, great fire-breathing dragons were seen in the sky towing huge Chinese junks behind them. According to legend, thousands of people witnessed these amazing sights.

Art by Matt DiPalma

In the 1930s the U.S. Navy operated two huge dirigibles, the *Akron* and the *Macon*. Each rigid airship was some 800 feet long. These great ships were unmistakable—their engines thundered as they flew overhead; millions of people witnessed their flights.   U.S. Navy photo

The Vought V173 experimental aircraft, derided by its pilots as a "flying flapjack," inspired thousands of UFO reports by startled witnesses.   U.S. Navy photo

The Approach Control Center for Raleigh-Durham Airport in
North Carolina. Many centers like this one have tracked
"bogeys"—targets on their scopes that could not be identified,
but were known not to be aircraft.   Photo by Michael Collins

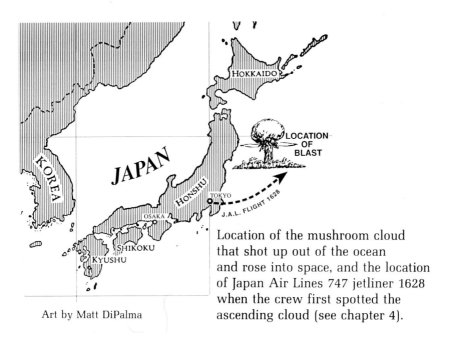

Location of the mushroom cloud that shot up out of the ocean and rose into space, and the location of Japan Air Lines 747 jetliner 1628 when the crew first spotted the ascending cloud (see chapter 4).

Art by Matt DiPalma

Former Air Force flight engineer and turret gunner Bert Perlmutter with his daughter at Teterboro Airport, New Jersey, before takeoff in a Flying Fortress bound for Boston.

Photo by Bill Mason

Ordinary film showed only the wooded area and marble bench. But a shot taken with infrared film simultaneously revealed a young woman seated on the bench. This is a rare example of a clear "ghost shot."   Photo by Dale Kaczmarek

Another example of infrared film capturing an image that remained invisible on regular film.

Photo by Dale Kaczmarek

Dame Sybil Leek, the "White Witch of England," was an astrologer who made incredible true predictions about *Apollo 13*'s flight, predictions that are still unexplained by science.

Photo courtesy of *Florida Today*

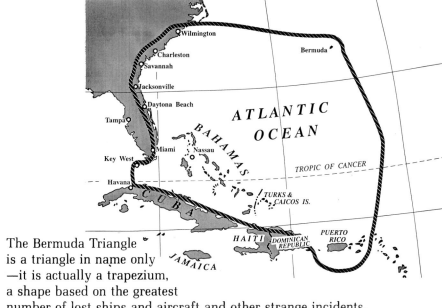

The Bermuda Triangle is a triangle in name only —it is actually a trapezium, a shape based on the greatest number of lost ships and aircraft and other strange incidents.

Art by Matt DiPalma

The mysterious vanishing of five Grumman TBF Avenger torpedo bombers like these in 1945 in the Bermuda Triangle has never been explained. No trace of the planes or their crews has ever been found.

U.S. Navy photo

Former Royal Air Force fighter pilot John Hawke was flying an Aztec on a ferry mission from Fort Lauderdale to Bermuda when, after passing out for one hour, he awoke several hundred miles from where his aircraft possibly could have flown in the meantime.   Photo by Bill Mason hands. Immediately the work crew began digging with a backhoe—and went straight to a deep aquifer of nearly thirty feet of sparkling spring water.

Dutchy Emery had accomplished in fifteen minutes with a forked branch what the most modern engineering equipment in the world had failed to do for twenty years.

Nowhere in the world has dowsing been as accepted as in the former Soviet Union. For decades the leading geological schools and laboratories of Moscow and Leningrad have not only studied dowsing but have used it as a working tool on the same level as their most advanced instruments. Leading much of this work has been Professor A. A. Ogilvy at Moscow State University, who brushed off unbelievers the world over with his declaration that the U.S.S.R. had made incredible advances in discovering the scientific basis of dowsing. He promised that with this solid new approach, dowsing "may well supplant contemporary geophysical methods in the search for water, ores, and petroleum products deep within the earth." Ogilvy added, "There's nothing mystical in the ability of men to react to underground sources of metallics or water."

Soviet scientists and geologists didn't only employ dowsers with reputed records of success—they took to dowsing themselves, mixing the still-unknown dowsing force with the sum of their own knowledge of geological formations. Hydrology professor G. Bogomolev and several assistants found to their surprise and elation that they were "natural dowsers," and soon they were recording not only the presence of subsurface water but also its depth. As they gained experience, they learned that certain variations in the way their forked branches moved indicated not water, but underground pipes and cables, and they perfected their system to such a degree that they were able to determine details down to the exact diameter of buried pipelines. Their first reports of success appeared in the January 1944 edition of the *Journal of Electricity*.

Water supplies were so critical during World War II that the Soviet army assembled more than a hundred soldiers, many of them engineers, gave them dowsing branches, and commanded them to go forth and "find electrical cables, water pipes, and seeping ground water."

The dowsing rods were forked branches from what is known in Russia as a shade tree, although the dowsers soon confirmed that forked branches from witch hazel, willow, or peach trees worked just as well. Underground wells and aquifers were located one after the other. Interestingly, it was found that women scored double the success rate as men in finding underground water as deep as 250 feet below the ground surface.

What was regarded in other countries as a dowsing rod became famed in the U.S.S.R. as a "wizard rod." After the war the Soviets accelerated their research and developed exacting methods for using their wizard rods to locate underground electrical wiring, plumbing, cables, and other "targets."

As restrictions of information exchange between countries eased and data flowed more readily, it was learned that S. Dokulil of Czechoslovakia had enjoyed "incredible success" with farm dowsing in his homeland. By 1961 he had been working for farmers' cooperatives with unquestioned success in locating sources for new wells for thirty-two years.

When Dr. Nikolai Sochevanov led a geological team through the Zabaikal and northern Kirgiz regions of Russia, he conducted dowsing experiments with several members of his group, including himself. They found water and mineral deposits while walking and flying over the regions.

Continuing his experiments, Sochevanov produced dowsing rods of steel, each rod starting with nearly five feet of one-eighth-inch-wide steel wire. He bent the wire into an eight-inch loop in the center and then extended the ends outward, six inches on each side, then down another twelve inches to form a U-shaped wizard rod. Finally he bent another three inches on the sides out to function as handles. To test his new wizard rod the geologist held the rod horizontally, his arms extended before him. To his delight, when he walked above water or minerals, the rods revolved at once.

The work of Sochevanov and other engineers led to major new physiological experiments in attempts to find out how and why the wizard rods worked the way they did. The new program was called "Biophysical Effect Method for Field Geology Research," an impressive title that simply means dowsing by humans. Their reports gathered "a tremendous amount of material: workers' journals and reports, variations in dowsing, and the physiological changes in the human operator."

It was discovered to the delight of dowsing researchers in other countries that these Soviet medical tests were very similar to work being carried out in the Netherlands and West Germany. There was growing evidence that the concept of a "sensing organ or system within the body" was simply not correct, and that successful dowsers reacted through their entire body rather than any one part or area. Professor J. Walther, of Halle, West Germany, reported that dowsers' blood pressure and pulse rates during the process of dowsing unquestionably rose well above the levels they experienced in other activities.

UNESCO teams didn't care who ridiculed their methods. Success was all that mattered. A Dutch geologist working with UNESCO, Dr. S. Tromp, came up with the surprising proof (as reported in the Winter 1968 *International Journal of Parapsychology*) that when the dowser's body reacted to water or minerals, his or her body also produced strong variations in cardiac functioning, which Tromp recorded with electrocardiograph readings.

The 1966 Moscow meeting of the All-Union Astro-Geodesic Society lasted for several days, fascinating scientists throughout Europe and drawing demands from across the world for copies of the proceedings. Two years later another Moscow conference reviewed the physiological aspects and consequences of dowsers at work. Again, the material was sought after eagerly by researchers from around the world. To read that dowsers were being used widely in Siberia's Yakut Republic, in Lithuania, in arid desert regions, and in the central Asian U.S.S.R. opened the door to new research in countries where dowsing had long been regarded suspiciously.

7

MONSTER MYTH, MONSTER REALITY

In 1924 in a mining camp bordering towering Mount Saint Helens in the northwestern corner of the United States, a group of miners walking within their camp stopped dead in their tracks. A man shouted in a voice unquestionably mixed with shock and fear. Heads turned to watch the man pointing with agitation toward a tree trunk. Everybody saw it, concealed partially behind the tree—a large creature that even at first glance appeared more apelike than human. Miners of that era, in rough country, were a tough lot and not easily put off. They lived with predatory animals all about them in the steep hills and woods.

There was something unreal behind that tree, as big as a bear and looking just as mean. In these men's minds you didn't try to merely scare off something that could possibly harm you. Immediately a miner snatched up a rifle and slammed a shot, dead-on. The bullet tore into the head of the strange creature. That should have been *that.*

It wasn't. The men stared, disbelieving, as the creature, instead of reeling back or slumping dead, spun about and ran off in a crazy ambling gait with surprising speed. Unfortunately, in the excitement of relating what happened, no one ever mentioned whether they examined the area for blood or pieces of bone, hair, or torn flesh. Whatever had taken a bullet to the head and run off full tilt was gone. Usually this meant just another great mountain tale to hand down for years to come, but this one wasn't yet ended.

Several days after the creature fled, another miner, Fred Beck, walked along a nearby canyon rim. He stopped short, with a grim set to his jaw, as he stared at another apelike creature.

Beck stared at the creature, it stared back, and as Beck lifted his rifle, the mysterious animal turned and ran swiftly away. Not quickly enough—Beck was fast with his rifle and a dead shot to boot. In rapid succession he pumped three bullets into the back of the fleeing creature. This time the bullets appeared to have their effect. The creature staggered, stumbled, and suddenly fell over the canyon edge into a long and terrible fall.

Having heard the shots, other miners rushed to join Beck. He related what had happened. With everybody armed to the teeth, the men clambered down into the canyon to examine the body. Without question it was dead. Three heavy rifle bullets into the back—nothing could survive that.

Yet there was no body, dead or alive, at the bottom of the canyon. No trace of the creature. The men were mystified. Murmurs of "ain't possible" grew into open questions of whether this thing was of our world—or had come "from the other side" and was more supernatural than previously suspected.

Once again, everyone figured the excitement was over. The miners returned to their cabin. They didn't even have time to finish their evening meal, as a swarm of the creatures rushed from the woods to hurl themselves at the cabin. The men bolted the door and everyone grabbed rifles as huge fists battered the door and walls. They heard the creatures clambering to the roof of their building, pounding madly against the thick beams above.

It was a night of fear and horror. The miners listened carefully to determine in exactly what spot the hammering went on, then loosed a barrage of rifle shots there. Dozens of rounds were expended, the inside of the cabin was acrid with smoke from the shooting, and *still* the battering continued. It went on all through the night, becoming increasingly worse as whatever it was outside began hurling heavy rocks at the cabin.

No one knows how many rifle shots were fired. There should have been apelike creatures, or pieces of them, splashed all over the roof and the ground about the cabin. With the onset of dawn the animals, if that is what they were, retreated into the thick woods and vanished.

The miners found not a single sign of any animal or human torn loose by their tremendous firepower.

That was enough for these men. They said to hell with the mines and everything else, jammed together their belongings, reloaded their rifles, and lost no time in abandoning the area.

Later, as he was questioned about these events, Fred Beck described the creatures as at least eight feet in height, weighing several hundred pounds, hairy, and massive in body. He also pointed out that they couldn't have been bears, as many listeners at first believed. As Beck noted sarcastically, "Damn bears don't throw no damn rocks."

Fred Beck and the others drifted into obscurity. Even the apelike creatures seemed to have melted for good into the remote woods. It took thirty years for them to show up again along distant areas of the northwest coastal area. By now the miners, no doubt with the assistance of news reporters, had nicknamed the creatures Bigfoot. Perhaps it helped to call them *something* other than "I ain't got no idea of what the hell it was."

Whatever these "Bigfoot" creatures were, they more than made up for their respite from clashing with humans. Reports began to flood local law offices and news media alike from miners, hunters, tourists, and local residents of the new communities that had advanced into former wilderness areas. Bigfoot, whoever and whatever, was emerging from the deep forests and mountain country and clearly on the loose again.

Yet the animals remained incredibly elusive to gunfire and almost impossible to capture on film. Some photographs were taken, of course, but many of them were

Polaroid-type shots that were excellent blurs and shadows and totally worthless. Better cameras, despite their advanced features, didn't do much better. And more and more people armed themselves with motion-picture cameras. Every now and then someone would come running to the public with sensational films of a huge, hairy creature either shambling along slowly or running away from the camera. Some were in color and lasted just long enough, judged the viewers, to "prove" once and for all the nature, size, and movement of the beasts.

They didn't prove much at all. Examination of the photographs and the film by skilled photographic interpreters left them full of doubt. Sufficient clarity was missing; without that clarity, the evidence simply couldn't be accepted as conclusive.

Well, that simply added fire to the growing number of news stories. In addition, there began to be confirmed reports of huge footprints in soft soil. People took off for the woods with more cameras, guns, and materials to make plaster casts of the foot imprints. Soon the newspapers and television featured the expected "adventurers" displaying close-up shots of their own bare feet alongside the much larger and impressive cast prints of Bigfoot. It proved one thing—whoever or whatever made those footprints was *big*. Unfortunately, a good many of the footprints were fake. Hoaxes sprang up like wildflowers as attention hunters displayed their stories to the media.

Arguments raged about the prints being those of huge bears or the elusive Bigfoot. Serious scientists and woodsmen cursed the hoaxers because they only turned an honest and vexing mystery into a muddle out of which no one seemed able to extract meaningful data.

And the reports kept coming in from the entire country! All of a sudden, Bigfoot, now endowed with all manner of exotic names and descriptions, was emerging from the undergrowth, mountains, and ravines of America, from Washington to Florida, from New England down to the Mexican border. The country was undergoing the strangest infestation of hairy creatures history had ever known. And now they were appearing in different sizes and shapes, with diverse facial characteristics and in varying colors.

Let it be understood, however, that this was not simply a barrage of nonsense. There *were* creatures of great size in the woods and fields. They were hairy, powerful, primitive in appearance and actions, and frustratingly human in certain characteristics. They exhibited varying levels of intelligence. The problem still lay in separating the truth from the hooey, but studies by veteran news reporters who wouldn't be fazed by the *Queen Mary* rolling along Highway 66 on roller skates brought acceptance by the doubters that something very strange was going on. The number of reliable, intelligent, capable witnesses, including many police officers, was now so great that the last shreds of doubt were pushed aside. The issue was to find out just what was going on—but in sufficient detail to make sense out of the growing clamor.

Because despite the reliability and number of the witnesses, the ability of the creatures to elude capture was even more baffling. People were out there in the woods and mountains with rifles that could drop an elephant in its tracks with a single shot. The creatures were somehow able to withstand the best of the firepower, and always vanished.

The creatures were being hit with everything from shotgun blasts to high-powered rifles, and the hits were multiple, and the creatures always survived and escaped. Perhaps they weren't really of this world. The speculation soared. Were they from a system of huge caves beneath the earth? Were they of so great a variety and size that they had been able all these centuries to avoid being hunted down and killed or captured?

Or did they exist in a dimension alongside our own and, through rifts in the fabric of time, move back and forth between Earth (ours) and Alternate Earth (theirs) when conditions were right? As strange and far-out and supernatural as *that* seemed, it retained a sort of permanence as a theory because *nobody* was hauling home a carcass on the hood of a pickup truck.

And by now the reported encounters were in the thousands.

What perplexed people more than anything else was the growing number of man-beast encounters and the startling variety of shapes, sizes, colors, and actions. Soon the reports were in the tens of thousands, and still Bigfoot, in his different shapes and names, continued to roam and wander and bound here and there with impunity.

The country, it seemed, was infested by things that shouldn't be able to exist, and we humans, who could take on even giant elephants with no more than spears, couldn't bring in something not that much larger than ourselves, even with the most powerful rifles ever made. It just did not add up. Something was crazy here, people felt. And they were right.

The deeper one studied the affair the greater the bafflement. What had these things been doing for so long? How had they bred in their isolation, how had they attended to nurturing and raising young, surviving storms and illness? How had they fended off predatory beasts armed with fang and claw? Above all, how had they managed for so many years at a time to avoid contact with humans?

There is no natural explanation in this world we know that would permit, under normal conditions, the existence of thousands of strange creatures throughout the world who seem to materialize out of nowhere, do what they do while they are here with all the solidity and reality of a water buffalo, and then utterly vanish, only to reappear somewhere else as if they had materialized out of nothing. Materialization and dematerialization is still heady stuff for even the most imaginative.

But experience leaves no doubt that there is something starkly unexplainable here.

THE DRAGON BONES

Somewhere in the misty beginnings of time, about two hundred thousand years ago, huge apes still wandered the lands of Asia. They were the largest apes known to science; their size has been confirmed at eight to ten feet tall. They were the last survivors of their kind, a hairy monster known as *Gigantopithecus* (which means literally gigantic ape). For the last several thousand years, fossil bones of this huge creature were found littering the landscape of southern China, and the Chinese, to whom fossils are dragon bones and dragon teeth, gathered them by the basketful to grind down into medicinal potions.

There seemed no end to the supply. Southern China is riddled with caves, and the caves obviously were once the homes of the great apes. More than seventy years ago a German researcher, Ralph von Koenigswald, wandered into a Chinese pharmacy and was astounded to see a huge fossil primate molar that didn't fit into any known catalogue. It was a molar from one of the extinct great apes; this find, among others, launched a storm of argument that these early primates were actually ancestors of modern man.

In 1956 Chinese scientists, working with Europeans, unearthed a huge complete jawbone. In a short time thousands of specimens were found. This enabled anthropologists to begin putting together a full-sized model of what this long-gone hairy creature looked like. The nearly complete jawbones of the "old one," when placed against the jawbone of a modern human, looked like a comparison between a fully grown adult human and a small child.

More recently, these same types of fossils have been found in other places. They began showing up in parts of Asia, Vietnam, Laos, Cambodia, and other areas, many of which were remote and jungle-covered. In the summer of 1992, scientists discovered a huge area of North Vietnam that had never previously been explored—and were astounded to find a startling array of animals and insects unknown to the rest of the world.

Samples of the ape fossils, and as much information as could be gathered, were brought to Bill Munns, who builds full-sized models of primates for display in zoos and schools. Munns could make such a realistic likeness that not even the living creature could tell it from the real thing.

When he was through, Munns presented his handiwork: brilliant, towering, lifelike—a giant that seems clearly to have lived in the same regions, at the same time, as our direct ancestors, *Homo erectus*, were living.

We know what a large male silverback gorilla adds up to in bulk, height, and basic characteristics. When the gorilla stands straight up he's a full six feet tall and can easily weigh in at four hundred pounds.

But *Gigantopithecus* makes that silverback look puny—when it stood erect it towered ten feet or more from toes to the top of its skull, and it averaged about 1,200 pounds. That's around the size of a very large male bear. There's still some argument as to whether the huge animals were quadrupedal, like the gorilla, or bipedal, like humans. They could have been either, and as additional evidence will illustrate, the odds seem to favor the human-like stance.

As intense and dedicated as the anthropologists were who studied *Gigantopithecus* and declared it extinct 200,000 years ago, they were wrong. The big creatures are still with us.

MONSTER REALITY

For years ex-U.S. Marine David E. Gower has had a nightmarish memory preying on his mind. It is so bizarre, so terrifying that he has refused to discuss what happened to him in Vietnam with anyone. After great effort he was persuaded finally to bring it to consciousness, to face the nightmare directly, so that he might not spend the rest of his life hiding from it. This information was made available for the first time in the form of a letter for this book in the late summer of 1992. The reader is left to place this episode in whatever perspective seems most suitable. . . .

In all the intervening years since I left Vietnam, I have lived with a memory that terrified me when it happened and seems no easier to live with today. I have never spoken of what happened except to share with my buddies who were with me at the time and were just as shook up as I was. It happened more than eighteen years ago when I was serving in 'Nam with the Fifth Special Forces Group, Marine Detachment.

We had pulled duty north of the DMZ [demilitarized zone], but that wasn't anything new to us. We'd been there before, and it wasn't an area where we would ever *want* to go. Our job was simple. "This is a search-and-destroy, ambush mission," was how we got the word. Like going down to the local bar for a few beers. It *sounded* like that from our mission leader's voice, but he knew just like the rest of us that it was a hornets' nest and not a bar toward which we were headed.

Well, up and out we went on a PBR [patrol boat, river], and the delivery boys in the PBR deposited us on an embankment some forty miles north of our starting point, on some who-cares, unnamed river in the middle of nowhere. It was what we called far out in East Jesus. The date was December 17, 1974.

The six-man group was under me. That means I was top dog, senior man, which also meant I'd usually be in the lead and was the most likely to get my head blown off or discover my stomach was being perforated. Specifically, we were to penetrate up to a distance of one mile into the jungle and then, at a preselected site, set up an ambush for the enemy with a medium machine gun. That weapon was my BAR, the Browning Automatic Rifle, solid and dependable and a bitch in combat. I had an M79 grenade launcher, one light machine gun (Thompson Subgun, caliber .45), and four M16 rifles in our group, with a *lot* of ammo. If the ambush worked, then we might be able to catch an NVA (North Vietnamese Army) ground supply convoy, moving with pack mules, headed south to the DMZ to reinforce enemy troops there.

The PBR was to take us upriver, drop us off, then move back downstream a distance of at least three hundred yards and wait under the cover of their camouflage nets and low-hanging branches. The plan was for them to wait for our signal by hand-carried radio, or, if they heard the uproar of a firefight under way, to get to us with heavier firepower. They'd blast their way upstream to the same point where they'd dropped us off. That gave us a definite rendezvous point, we'd be able to bring all our firepower together in a concentrated effort, and, if we ran into more than we could handle, then would be the moment for what is officially called emergency evacuation, but which for us was "let's get the hell out of here—NOW!"

Let me make it clear—we didn't have any rowboat to mess around with. In other words, ours wasn't the standard PBR. In addition to the three M60 machine guns on board, there was also a twin-mount .50-caliber machine gun in the forward deck with anti-frag shields around it. And on the sides of the pilothouse we had belt-fed grenade launchers. And to top it off on the after-deck we had a pair of twenty-millimeter rapid-fire cannon in anti-aircraft mounts. All in all, it was an absolutely devastating package of firepower. We could destroy a small town if we had to with all that stuff.

It was comforting to know we weren't the usual lightly armed floating target the enemy loved to work over. And to add just a bit more for extra value, we brought along one sixty-millimeter mortar. Now, that mortar was really a killing machine, but it had its own problems, which centered around how we were going to mount that thing solidly to the boat deck. We let the PBR guys wrestle with the problem; if you want to stay alive in this business you concentrate on what's going to be coming after you.

We went upriver in darkness. By 0130 [1:30 A.M.] we were at the ambush area. I told my troops to saddle up and that we were going ashore in five minutes. Right on time, the cox'n, or boat driver as the marines called them, brought the PBR keel to the spongy soil with a touch that belied his bulk and hamlike fists. It was like an easy stop in an elevator.

We hit the shore with each of us carrying a light pack and the much heavier weapons. From the instant we touched ground I was uncomfortable. The footing underneath was really a bitch; it was spongy, and in some areas the mud or ground beneath our feet was like the black earth found in a Louisiana bayou. This was the kind of sucking mud that could get us into trouble fast, impeding our movement just when we might need speed. Instead of going south as planned, I directed our team northward. The immediate bank was very steep with thick undergrowth, and the growth appeared to continue some distance inland. We didn't discover until later that it was thick, cloying jungle, not just riverbank growth.

Out on the river, the moon had never been brighter. We were able to read by that silvery light. But once we got into dense jungle I could barely see twenty feet before us. We went through about a hundred yards of this maze, then it thinned a bit, and to our surprise we broke through into an unexpected clearing.

Immediately we began spreading out. Going across open ground, bunched together, is an invitation to disaster. The hairs on the back of my neck felt like they were crawling. There was something *strange* about this area. I couldn't pin it down but I was hair-trigger alert, much more so than usual.

There wasn't a sound, and that was wrong. It seemed none of the animal life, or even the usual plague of insects, would come out into the open. I figured this was my imagination, because what the hell could bother insects?

Yet that sense of *strange* wouldn't go away. We all made sure our weapons were ready to fire in an instant. The feeling of *strange* steadily went to *bad*.

Try to understand something about where we were and what was happening. In bush country, there are *always* bugs and small animals scurrying about. If they stop moving because you're passing close by them, they wait a few seconds until the danger is gone and very quickly resume their incessant night noise.

But not now. Not in this area. It was like an abandoned cemetery.

I motioned for Lance Corporal Terry to move up to scout the area a few hundred meters ahead of us. Terry had been raised in the back country of northern Georgia and he was the perfect scout. He could have been an Indian, he was so quiet. I had seen him slip up to a tree and swat birds off limbs; they never knew he was coming. He could be scary at times, moving like a wraith. Right now it was good to know he could move anywhere and not be detected.

We'd been in this clearing area about twenty

minutes when I sent Terry ahead to scout for us. He was back in five minutes. "Man, there ain't nothing alive or moving within thirty meters of this damn clearing," he told me. "And there ain't no tracks I could find, no animal trails leading off into the bush. *Nothing.* And nothing a human foot would make. Not a single footprint anywhere. This place is crazy."

"How do you feel about it?" I asked him.

"Scary," came the answer, and that only heightened my own growing sense of fear. Something was *wrong.* Terry didn't fear anything that walked, crawled, swam, or flew. Nothing. He was the best man I could ever want out in the bush. We'd had an agreement a long time that if one of us ever got wounded badly, the other would always carry or drag him out.

You had to see Terry in action to really understand this. He was only five feet, five inches tall, and every inch was pure hate. He weighed 135 pounds, all of it spring steel and viciousness. We were a great team. He was tough to handle but he also knew that if he got out of line I'd shoot his young ass and leave him for lunch for the bugs. We weren't what you call buddies, but we absolutely counted on one another in combat. Terry was one of the finest marines with whom I'd ever served in combat.

By now, Terry had circled the entire clearing, his senses almost on fire he was so hopped up with that feeling of *wrong.* He'd gone through 250 meters of clearing and came back to me shaking his head. "Man, there ain't *nothing* here. Nothing that any human being ever left here either. And that ain't right."

Everybody was starting to get edgy. All Terry had found was a strange fecal deposit on the ground. He could tell the difference between the droppings of a goat and of a sheep, but this time he was baffled. "It don't fit," he said slowly. "It just does not *fit*." Fingers nervously caressed triggers as the minutes went by. Yet, finding some strange droppings shouldn't have bothered anyone. Not in this damned country where the jungle was full of everything from tiny mice to huge tigers.

We'd been within the clearing for perhaps ten to fifteen minutes when I heard—or detected— movement through the bushes well in front of us. I gave the high sign. Immediately Terry moved about twenty feet to my right. Salazar slipped away behind me, slightly off to one side, about a distance of ten feet.

We'd learned long ago, the hard way, about silence in the bush. The lessons had been learned at the cost of friends now dead. So when we stopped, if we were near a rock, then we became a part of that rock. If near a bush, we became a part of the bush. If a person who wore glasses kept his face tilted downward, even on a bright night, he'd prevent any reflection that could be seen from a distance.

By now we were sure we'd made the contact that we needed. We wanted to get our work done and get the hell out of there, head back south again.

I want to explain we'd been in combat more times than we cared to remember. When we joined this outfit, the Fifth Group, we just gave ourselves up for dead. It made more sense than it seems. We'd all become intimate with the expression, "A dead man is hard to kill," and while that sounded like it had philosophical overtones, we never really knew what it meant. Until this night, that is.

Whatever was out there in the bush, it wasn't

trying to conceal its presence. There were a lot of them, whoever they were, or else we were dealing with something large and clumsy like a water buffalo. The animal, or group of enemy, was skirting the clearing just as we had. Making sure not to expose itself. Finally we saw unmistakable movement of the bushes as whatever was out there began to move straight at us. And when we saw what was coming we'd gladly have settled for a tiger or even a whole damn herd of buffalo.

Because I'll never forget that night as long as I live.

There were at least three of them. At least three that I saw.

As gyrenes go I'm a good-sized combat dude. I'm well over six feet, two inches with plenty of hulk to go with the height. I say this because I judge the height of others very well. What appeared before us was a hell of a lot bigger than myself. I estimated a minimum of seven feet tall, one at least eight feet or taller, and *the damn things were bright yellow.*

Yellow all over them. With a crazy diffused outline, like watching a movie shot with a soft-focus lens.

As they came closer I could see they had large three-digit hands, with what I swear were four-inch claws on the ends.

I couldn't make out the faces very well, with the outlines broken up the way they were, but to my best recollection, to which is added details specified by the other guys, the things appeared to have two eyes, some sort of nose slit on flat faces, and audio holes on the upper part of the sides of their heads.

That is, if you could imagine these things out of Hell as having *faces.*

One of the problems was the yellow light

that seemed to be generated by these . . . well, I'll just call them Big Yellows. The light was unholy, unmistakable. The more clearly I saw the Big Yellows, the more I began to realize they were huge, on the verge of being massive.

They were moving slowly across the clearing, and as they began passing us I realized I'd been holding my breath and I was going to suffocate if I didn't suck in air. At the same time I was afraid to on the chance that such a sudden gasp of air would alert these things to our presence.

I held out long enough, like the other guys, until the three Big Yellows moved back into the bushes. Terry and I moved forward carefully to inspect the ground for any tracks these things might have left. Sure enough, there they were. Three-toed tracks. Toes or digits, I don't know, but it was the same as the hands.

After studying the tracks, we just stood there staring at each other for what seemed like long minutes. In reality I guess it must have been only twenty seconds or so. I said to Terry, "Screw this. Let's go back." And we started the return to our troops.

At this point I don't know what Terry was thinking, but my own mind was a blank. Jeez, what we'd seen *didn't exist*, and they'd passed by almost close enough to touch.

A child can accept things like Batman, Superman, and all kinds of superheroes, but *not* a thinking adult. We've all been taught since we were old enough to understand words that everything has to fit neatly within its own little pigeonhole. "They," whoever or whatever "they" may be, also have to follow the rules. "They" may even be omnipotent, but rules are rules, and what we had just seen wasn't in the rulebooks. Common sense was shouting at me in the back of my skull that what I'd seen could not exist. Finally I shut down all the self-arguing and figured I'd better just get everybody the hell out of there while the getting was good.

We were just back into the bushes on the same side of the clearing we'd come into during our trek from the boat. Then my blood turned cold. Those things, the Big Yellows, were coming back toward us and this time at a dead run! The ground pounded as though elephants were in a stampede.

"Back to the river!" I shouted. "Salazar! Get on that damn radio and tell 'em we're coming out hot!"

I'll tell you right out that I was a husky gyrene in damned good physical condition and I was two hundred pounds of conditioned muscle. I'll also tell you right out that never in my life did I ever move as fast as I did that night. With my full pack and weapons I was running just as fast as my legs could move and I think they were a blur. I went leaping over fallen trees and bushes like a hyped-up Olympic hurdler, but everyone else was in the lead and I was bringing up the rear. Jesus!

To hell with keeping quiet! We all knew we were running for our lives, and that if we stopped something was going to have us for lunch. I know, it's crazy. We had incredible firepower with us and we were all veterans of combat, and we believed absolutely that—until this moment—we'd tackle anything on earth and whip ass all the way. It wasn't until later that I realized my thoughts had snagged on that phrase of "anything on earth." What I'd seen looking right back at me wasn't anything known on this earth.

I kept hearing a wheezing kind of growl getting closer with every step. I knew if I didn't make a decision to turn and at least try to kill it with the BAR, which would chew a tiger to shreds, then this thing might just get us all. Starting with me. And like I'd said before, the smell of death was all over us, and in those moments you fall back on the canard that a dead man not only is hard to kill, but he sure hasn't a thing to lose by what he does.

I knew I was going to die. And that was crazy! Fully armed, deadly, I was running away without yet having fired a shot and I flat knew I was going to die. It was like an invisible arrow had smacked into my brain with that message, it was so strong. Then instinct and training (and maybe longtime bad manners) took over, and I figured I'd start doing some damage of my own.

I always had that BAR "cocked and locked." I always had a round in the chamber and the weapon on safe and carried at high port arms. That is, while running, it was almost chest high across the front of my body.

Another completely crazy thing happened. I could "feel" the thing's hot breath on my back. But that was impossible! I was wearing a full pack at the time, so . . .

Then the moment came. I thought, *this is it, man,* and I cut left as hard as I could and spun around, and promptly fell on my ass. But my weapon was up to my chest, almost to my shoulder, and almost on target. The Big Yellow *had turned with me.* There was a swishing sound where a deadly set of claws ripped right through where I would have been had I kept running. I mean literally that those massive arms and claws were stirring up a wind in the still air of the jungle.

But now I was on target, the weapon off safe, and I moved into a half-rise position; instantly I felt better when my trigger finger closed.

I was less than twenty-five feet from the thing when I fired. I couldn't miss. I was an experienced sniper, and I'd been through special schools at Camp LeJeune where I'd proved my ability long before this moment. In short, I was dead-on.

Big Yellow was still full on its feet after taking a direct hit from a .30-caliber round from a machine gun.

By now I was standing and the thing was facing me. I thought I could make out some kind of fangs, like the larger canines of some large dog, but with the wildness of the moment I won't swear to details like that. But I'll never forget those snakelike eyes and canines.

That moment will forever be in the nightmares I've had since that day. Like I said, it was as if something penetrated my mind, just as my round had slammed into Big Yellow.

What I said after getting Big Yellow with a direct hit, and that thing not even being bothered, was—I was told later—some award-winning profanity.

We stood like that a timeless moment, then it started after me again, making that snuffling kind of growling sound. But I'd had enough.

There I was in a gloomy jungle, this kind of eternal twilight, having blasted this creature, and it starts moving toward me again. I don't know why I just stood there staring open-mouthed at it.

That can't be true. Of course I know *why* I did that! I could not believe that anything that breathed could withstand a 30.06 round up close. I always loaded my magazines myself for anything weird we might run into. The first round was a 30.06 armor-piercing round, my second was a Spire point, the third was a Boattail, then back to armor-piercing, then Lead-Nose jacketed, and more armor-piercing rounds. Any man loaded like that is a killing machine of the worst kind, and that was me. With that kind of mag load you can bring down *anything*.

I think Big Yellow might have stumbled a bit. But only once when I'd hit him.

So I figured this mother was going to eat everything I had to offer. Like 180 grains of jacketed .30-caliber rounds, and my finger came back on the trigger.

I had twenty rounds for that big dude. And I was dead-on, point-blank range, and I squeezed off round after round, and I hit that son of a bitch again and again—and again. I didn't jerk the rounds like a man frightened as badly as I was might do. Instinct and training always pays off, and at this business I was all professional. I put each round carefully into Big Yellow's chest, and I saw it jerk backward, at times convulsively, with each new hit, and I was counting off every round.

Now that I was firing, all fear had left me. I was *killing*, and I was never bothered with fear when I was blasting away. It was pure killing drive, and those rounds could have pulped the head and horns of the biggest damn water buffalo that ever lived and left it a headless water buffalo even before it went down.

It just stood there, twitching, while I pumped round after round, every one of them dead-on, into its chest.

On round nineteen I switched to fire at its head. Figured I'd put one right between its eyes into the brain.

The BAR just clicked.

Good God! I had a dead primer on that round!

I figured I was dead. Big Yellow was starting after me as though I had never even touched it. There was only one thing left for me to do and that was to run like hell.

I ran. Faster than before. The BAR couldn't stop that thing. *Get the hell out!* my own mind was screaming at me.

I was heading for where I knew the patrol boat would be out in the river. There it was, just pulling away from the riverbank when I saw it through the brush.

That was an immense relief, but very short-lived. I could hear Big Yellow gaining on me. I'd already figured on going swimming, which is the same as hurling myself as far as I could into the river to get to the PBR if it was off-bank, but when I saw the boat right before me I ran even faster and then leaped wildly for the deck.

I felt something go *smack!* at one shoe when I leaped. When I hit the deck with a crash, I fell on my left side with my legs tangled and against the frag shield of the fifty-caliber.

It's amazing how fast you can judge things when you're terrified. It took barely a second to realize that I was back on the PBR and Big Yellow was *still* coming after me. I yelled to the crewman to aim at the area with his fifties—right where I'd come through the brush—aim and "Open fire, damn it!"

I ran back to one of those powerful twenty-millimeter cannon anti-aircraft guns, all the time screaming to the cox'n to get the hell out into the river. I was only distantly aware there was already a gunner on the big twenty-millimeter, but without thinking I grabbed him to hurl him out of the way so I could handle that weapon myself. My BAR was still on the deck—useless to me.

Then, except for engine roar, water sounds,

and muttering, it was amazingly quiet. Everybody had their weapons trained into the brush in case those things decided to come on over and play.

The lead creature stayed concealed. *For a while . . .*

We were going downriver, but still in sight of that area where we'd come dashing back to the PBR. Suddenly seven of us watched the riverbank area shimmer—a great spray of yellow expanding outward like a silent explosion of yellow fog. We were stunned.

We couldn't make out if they'd all come to the edge of the clearing, or if there was only one. But it was nighttime, it was dark, damn it—and we were watching an incredible yellow glow. No way to tell any numbers of the things.

And we didn't care. We wanted out and we went to full throttle and everybody kept their weapons trained on that yellow shining fog until we rounded a river bend and kept going.

One of the boat crew asked if we'd seen that "tiger" that appeared on the bank where we were moving out. (I never knew of a tiger that would run *into* heavy gunfire. . . .) Those of us who'd been ashore looked at one another in a long silence and we knew better than to make a report of what we'd actually seen. The headshrinkers would be all over us like fleas on a bleeding dog. "Tiger" would do fine. One or two of my patrol just nodded.

Now I had time to reflect. Tensions were easing among the crew, but I noticed they still had their weapons at the ready to open fire on just about anything. You talk about being spooked, and that was us. But at least I could think now.

I went over details in my mind while everything was fresh. Then we heard a wild animal roar from where we'd been, and I'll tell you right now, I've seen tigers, I've heard tigers, I'd had face-to-face meetings with tigers, and *that* was no tiger.

The sound made me stumble on the boat deck. I looked down to my boots. The heel on the right boot was missing. Salazar saw me staring at my boot. His gaze followed mine and then he went pale.

Powerful claws had torn the heel from the boot. I sort of retreated into myself on the PBR until we got back to Camp Bearcat.

I didn't sleep that night. I couldn't. That face straight out of Hell, the claws and the savagery, and that inhuman yellow glowing light . . . well, it was too much. I didn't sleep for four days straight until I stumbled about like a zombie. Finally on the fifth day I passed out from physical exhaustion. Incredibly, no nightmares. When I awoke I "knew" that thing wouldn't be coming after me in the dark. But until then? I was absolutely convinced I was going to have to fight that thing to the death, that we were joined together in some unholy struggle. Then that went away.

For a time I even tried to rationalize that the whole thing had been a dream. No way—it was all too stark, there were all the other witnesses, there was the power and shock of snapping out rounds with the BAR—and there was that missing right heel that had been torn off and the gouge marks from claws that, by actual measurement of my boot, were two and three-quarter inches wide.

Sometimes a different realization sets in slow. There was a thing out there that was capable of taking eighteen 30.06-caliber ammunition rounds—armor-piercing, jacketed, lead, everything—right into its chest and all it did was sort of twitch a bit and grumble, *and then* come hell bent for leather after me at a dead run.

There is nothing that exists in this world that

can do *that*. We seven never spoke of it again. We told a few close friends at first. They either didn't believe us or they didn't want to believe us, so we said to hell with them and everyone else, and until I got pushed and threatened by one of my best friends, who's authoring this book, I'd figured I'd *never* talk about it again. And the only reason I'm doing it now is that the things I've seen and learned with this friend can widen your eyes as big as saucers. *I trust him*; that's why you're reading this now.

I'm the only one left of that patrol. The other six are gone, and they took their secret with them to the grave. We left five of them dead in the paddies of 'Nam; the other one died in a car crash back in the States. Hell of a way to go after being one of only two combat survivors of our marine outfit.

For years, keeping my reasons to myself, I've tried to find some reference to anything that could have tied in to what I've called Big Yellow. For years I studied every book that applied, in every library of every ship to which I was assigned, at marine bases, at terrific government research facilities. I went after everything from anthropological to the supernatural. Then, just a few years back, I came straight up in my seat. I'd finally found something.

I was studying a book titled *The Tomb* by F. Paul Wilson. I was amazed. Wilson's descriptions of strange and terrible creatures described what I'd seen in Vietnam almost perfectly. I wondered if he had ever seen them personally. I wrote him, tried to call him, badgered his publisher to contact him. Zero. Nothing.

But now, for the reasons I've given, here I am, here is what happened, and I still go icy cold when I think of the savagery and the ability of a creature to take eighteen rounds of perfectly aimed point-blank fire into the chest from a BAR.

Neither human nor animal can withstand that. You see, that kind of firepower just doesn't hit a physical body and tear inside. It makes a nine-millimeter autofire, which is a hell of a weapon, like a BB gun in comparison. The muzzle velocity of the BAR and the variety of ammo tears out great chunks of flesh, explodes bones; *it destroys.*

So it wasn't, of course, human.

And I'll tell you right now it wasn't animal as we know the word.

I don't give a damn *what* bones they found in Asia, or what models the anthropologists have built, no matter what resemblance is involved.

You ever see a kodiak bear? They get up to 1,500 pounds and they make a grizzly, by comparison, look about the size of a large dog.

That BAR, with its ammo, would have blown any kodiak into bits, pieces, chunks, and bloody spray.

Big Yellow twitched, grunted, and came on after me.

Whatever it is, and I've begun to learn just how possible is this concept they call the Doorways, it also glows in the dark, it has some physical features no other animal has. . . . well, I can't tell you any more than you've read in these pages.

But it isn't, and it never will be, *natural.*

8

LIVING MEMORIES AND
OLD FRIENDS

There are ghosts aboard airplanes and trains, in houses, and on ships at sea. Sailing's past has no shortage of bloodcurdling tales, most with no proof and many leaving more questions than answers.

But it is one thing to have ghosts moving through the great old sailing ships, and quite something else to have a poltergeist raising its own devilry in one of the most modern great fighting ships of the world.

That was the chilling reality of life aboard the USS *Forrestal* aircraft carrier of the U.S. Navy—not simply a ghost, but a troublemaker who not only jangled nerves and messed up equipment, but also put in appearances seen by hundreds of crewmen!

When you live aboard a floating city and there's nowhere to go to get away from it all, as many sailors and officers finally judged, you may as well get friendly with whatever it is that is haunting you. Being frightened didn't do any good, and trying to ignore the poltergeist was impossible. So someone one night called him "George," the name spread swiftly through the ship, and from that night on, George it was.

When the stories first began to circulate through the fleet, listeners smiled and indulged the men who related what was going on aboard *Forrestal*. After all, pilots are famous for their good-luck charms and their superstitions, so almost everyone figured that the ghost was really just some crewmen being spooked during moments of danger, and said ghost was probably wandering about the flight

deck, maybe even hooting along with the roar of jet engines and snarl of propellers.

But that wasn't the case at all. George apparently
couldn't have cared less what they had up on deck. Airplanes or trucks, it didn't matter to him. George, witnesses
swore, hung around the below-the-waterline sections of
the aircraft carrier known as the number-one and number-
three "holes"—carrier jargon for the huge areas where
pump rooms, storerooms, and the freeze lockers (also
called reefers) for frozen food are. Go to the number-one
hole, which has the biggest reefers on *Forrestal*, and just
about any man on board will tell you, "Look out for
George. He likes that place particularly." A pleasant
enough invitation to meet a ghost, until the new men
aboard *Forrestal* discovered that number-one forward, as
Lieutenant James E. Brooks reported, "is also the ship's
morgue."

Yet the old-timers weren't put off by ghosts, poltergeists, or any out-of-this-world visitations. Chief Warrant
Officer Otha Davis, the cargo and food service division
officer for *Forrestal*, had no reservations about his attitude. "If there's a ghost down there, then I want to know
about it," he said tersely. "Because if there *is*, I want to put
him to work!" Davis also made it plain to all concerned he
just didn't believe in ghosts aboard the aircraft carrier. But
the stories had their use to him. "When the executive
officer asks me about a zone inspection discrepancy," he
laughed, "I always blame it on George."

Lieutenant Brooks made it just as clear that there were
plenty of *Forrestal* crewmen who thought otherwise. Reporting events from the aircraft carrier in special assign-
ment to *Naval Aviation News*, Brooks wrote that crewmen
"who have worked in these spaces don't share Davis's
disbelief of a ghost on the 1,039-foot supercarrier." Brooks
gathered reports from members of the crew and quoted
Mess Specialist First Class Daniel Balboa who worked in
both number-one and number-three holes.

"When I first came aboard in January 1985," Balboa

stated, "I was a little apprehensive about the things I heard. I thought everyone was pulling my leg. We had problems keeping the reefer doors closed. They always seemed to be opening up. The engineers who monitor temperatures in the reefers blamed the mess specialists. We blamed them. One night, I went down to take temperatures myself. As I worked from one reefer to the next [you must traverse one to get to the next], I closed the door behind me. Fifteen minutes later, when I turned to leave, all three doors were open."

Could Balboa have been *that* careless or forgetful? "It was impossible for anyone to open the reefer doors from the outside, behind me," Balboa added. "Opening them from the outside requires a key, since the doors lock automatically. I had the only key. That incident put me on the verge of believing.

"I told some other guys what happened and one of the engineers said that when he was climbing the ladder out of number-one pump room below the reefers, something grabbed his leg and pulled down. When he turned around and looked, nobody was there."

According to the reports gathered from crew members, the ghost named George seemed drawn to Balboa, and when Balboa entered number-three hole, George was right on the spot. "I was taking inventory one night," Balboa explained, "and heard a noise like deck grating being picked up and dropped. I turned around and looked but didn't see anything. When I returned to my work, the noise started again."

After this happened another three times, other crewmen developed an aversion to entering number-three hole. "I've got one guy working for me," Balboa added, "who refuses to go down there alone. I've never seen any ghosts, but you can hear weird things down there."

Other crewmen received "special attention" from George. James Hillard was assigned to duties in cargo from April 1986 to April 1987. One night he was moving frozen foods out of the reefer when suddenly the lights flickered on and off. Hillard believed another shipmate to be playing tricks on him with the light switches, but that man denied he had even touched the light switches. Then the lights snapped out again. They were in darkness. Something or someone rapped him on his shoulder. The lights flashed on again, giving Hillard time to see his shipmate standing much too far from the light switches to have flipped them one way or another.

Then George went on a haunting binge for more crewmen working number-one and number-three holes. Isolated incidents increased to almost daily events. The entire ship's crew began to take notice as the on-and-off light switching spread to other areas and the metal gratings echoed to the unmistakable sounds of footsteps when no one was walking along them (at least not anyone who could be seen). At work one day, Hillard and several other men were transferring supplies when a shipboard telephone began ringing. One man answered the phone, but no one was at the other end. It rang again after he hung up. Again, no one was there. After this happened several more times, Hillard told the crewman to disconnect the phone, and then shouted to crewmen working above him. "You guys trying to call me?" he asked. A clear "No!" came back.

The disconnected phone rang again and this time Hillard grabbed it. "There was a faint voice calling, 'Help! Help! I'm on the sixth deck!' Well, rumor had it that a crew member was killed there. I'm very scared to go there alone. If I do," he added ruefully, "I get out as fast as I can."

Again there was a change. George became visible to several crewmen, including Hillard, who related, "I was working cargo in number-three hold on the fourth deck. A buddy and I sat down to take a break. We heard someone walking on the deck grates. I looked out in the passageway and saw someone walk by about five feet away. He was wearing a khaki uniform like an officer or chief would wear. He went into the spice rack. I waited a few minutes for him to come out. When he didn't, I went in to take a look. There was nobody in there, and I swear that is where he went."

Soon after, Gary Weiss watched the khaki-uniformed ghost clamber down a ladder to pump room number one. Weiss swears that whoever went down the ladder never came up again, and when he personally checked the pump room, there was no one else there. And the ladder was the *only* access to the room.

Rumors and speculation became the chief subject of conversation with many men aboard *Forrestal*. Who was "George"? Did he have any former connection with the great aircraft carrier? Someone recalled the terrible fire that had raged along the flight deck back in 1967. One hundred and thirty-seven men died in the inferno. Names were brought up, in particular one chief petty officer. Then someone offered the memory of a pilot who was killed during a flight. His body was recovered, brought aboard *Forrestal*, and then stored in the reefer until it could be removed from the warship. There wasn't any way to be certain of the identity of the ghost, but the name George, most men agreed, was an incidental reaction to recalling that the former cargo division officer was Lieutenant George Conway.

Jeff Scott, Dave Goeddertz, Brett Reynolds, and Napoleon Hayes had more encounters with George than rapping sounds or ghostly echoes. The most frightening incident took place in a reefer room when a heavy stack of beef suddenly fell and jammed the reefer door shut, trapping the men inside. When questioned about the incident, they all agreed that the beef had been stacked securely against the wall near the door and had been there at least a week. But it fell over and jammed the door not in rough seas, but when the winds were calm, as was the sea, and there was no one outside the reefer who could have shoved the heavy beef in any direction.

No one ever pinned down George the ghost, but they didn't stop his wanderings and inexplicable pranks. Locked doors swing open by themselves, crewmen hear footsteps along gratings while the gratings are in full view and there is no one to be seen. The electricians become weary of being called to repair lights that snap off and on.

USS *Forrestal* is one of the mightiest warships in the
world, an efficient, powerful combat veteran. Its crew is
changed regularly.

Except for George.

Sometimes a ship, small or as large as a huge aircraft
carrier, becomes the center of a moment that seems separated from all normal time and space. There is no frantic
excitement, no roar of battle, but a presence—then an
appearance that can chill the blood.

One man who experienced such a moment is David K.
Bowman, who served nearly twenty-five years in the U.S.
Navy until he retired. Bowman served on active duty from
1968 through most of 1970 off the coast of Korea on the
USS *Oriskany*, an aircraft carrier itself retired from active
duty and mothballed in Bremerton, Washington.

Dave Bowman's "moment" is chilling to the extreme,
and he underplays a terrifying encounter with his own,
quiet title—

BLACKOUT EXERCISE OFF KOREA

One of the spookiest things I've ever experienced
was the blackout exercise I went through on
board the aircraft carrier USS *Oriskany* off the
coast of Korea in September 1970. Every light
that could possibly be seen from outside the ship
was extinguished; this meant that the only illumi-
nation available anywhere in the ship, except for
deep within the vessel, were blood-red night
lights spaced along the decks in passageways
every ten feet or so. Some passages didn't have
any lights.

It was after flight operations and the entire
carrier task force was steaming through a gray
dusk as I finished jogging on the flight deck. I did
this on many nights for the exercise after spend-
ing the day cooped up in the VF-194 squadron

administration office. I noticed right away that something was different; the various destroyers and cruisers steaming in position around our ship were just dark silhouettes with an occasional red light glimmering through the haze. Going below for dinner, I saw right away that our ship, too, was "blacked out." An aircraft carrier is dangerous enough when there is light, but in complete darkness there is hazard everywhere. Carefully, I felt my way down totally darkened passageways. It was slow going as I eased my way across catwalks with narrow rails and down steep ladders, descending a total of five decks to get to the so-called main deck located two decks below the hangar deck. On that deck, at least there were red night lights; an occasional figure passed me in the eerie red gloom as other men went about their business.

About twenty feet ahead, a passageway came from the entrance to the mess decks on my left to form a T intersection. A few feet before that, in the deck, yawned a small hatch leading down to the berthing spaces.

As I approached the T intersection, an extremely tall, almost cadaverous figure, dressed in dungarees and a white hat, appeared from the left, seemingly with one step. He stood for a moment facing me, illuminated by a red night light, his eyes wide and staring, *but with no pupils visible, just whites.* Just as suddenly, he took another large step to my left and disappeared down the hatch into the berthing compartment.

I stood for a few long seconds in the red half-darkness and then did something that I didn't think I could ever do under such circumstances.

I followed the strange figure down the hatch.

But on the next deck below, there were only sleeping men on bunks, red night lights, the quiet whine of turbines far below. I almost couldn't believe it. I went down the ladder to the next deck and it was the same thing: softly snoring men, red lights, the distant whining of machinery.

It was at that moment that I immediately asked myself what the hell I was doing chasing a phantom through dark berthing compartments and, not wasting a moment, I whipped back up the two ladders and around the corner and down the huge double-wide ladder into the mess decks, where there were bright lights, people, the sounds and smells of the evening meal.

To this day, I am not certain what I saw that night long ago. But I don't think it was "normal," whatever that means. And it has occurred to me more than once that whoever walks the decks of ships in blackout exercises . . . may not walk alone.

It is frustrating to read about ghosts—ghosts sworn to by good men and women, considered paragons of truth, virtue, and honesty. Ghosts seen again and again. Ghosts heard, ghosts angry, ghosts friendly. But every story that rolls down the passageways of history can be taken for no better than it is—carrying a burden of fright, emotion, hallucination, and desire. We are left with detailed stories of such encounters, but not a shred of proof. For such moments lie beyond proof. In our era of science, technology, electronics, and computers, proof means being able to repeat or replay any moment or incident sworn to be real. Without that hook on which to hang the moment for examination and dissection, scientists dismiss ghost stories with contempt.

As Loyd Auerbach said so pointedly, there have never been any good pictures of ghosts. Cameras of all kinds, including regular, Polaroid, motion-picture, and video, have been used to attempt to "catch" ghosts, and still the ghosts remain elusive. Pictures *do* exist, but they are fuzzy, hazy, and almost always unfocused when examined by technicians using digitized computer techniques to discover the flaws and errors that clearly mark a fraud or a hoax.

But there *are* pictures that defy the experts, even if many of them—honestly taken and sworn to—remain in the category of strange lights, ghostly images, glowing forms. It is not up to the experts, however, to prove the reality and accuracy of the pictures, but to disprove them.

There is one method that troubles all concerned with capturing ghosts—photography taken with infrared film. Infrared film records what is seen only in the infrared part of the spectrum, which is invisible to the human eye. One photographer reported, for example, that when taking a series of shots of a cemetery (and no one was there except the photographer), the shots were made in a double series, one with regular film and the other with infrared film. Using regular film the photographer got the results he expected—excellent pictures of the area he wished to capture. But the photograph taken of the exact same area with infrared film stunned the photographer—there was a young woman seated on a marble bench! He compared both pictures, one alongside the other, and the results were unmistakable. The young woman is visible only on the infrared film (see photo insert).

A second example in the photo insert, which is grainy because of major enlargement, was another shocker. Again, the area was being swept by the photographer for a series of shots of a wooded park area. And again, both types of film were being used for the special effects desired. The infrared picture showed a young woman walking through the woods. She was not visible in the pictures where regular film was used.

Sooner or later the question of proof cries for attention. This presents an all-too-familiar situation—the photographer is competent, reliable, and honest and doesn't try to create a financial bonanza from the photographs. The photos are sought desperately by researchers trying to unravel the mystery of why the "ghosts," if that is what they are, reflect light in the infrared part of the spectrum, but not in visible light. Everyone involved will vouch for the facts—how and when the photographs were taken, processed, and printed—but it simply will not do for the hard-nosed scientist and/or researcher who refuses to personally or professionally attest that everything involved with these photographs is genuine. And this is a sound position to take. *Photographs are not proof.* They are fascinating, interesting, instructive, but not *proof* as science defines the term.

Hundreds of these "ghost" photographs have confounded photographers and viewers alike. Some are taken in black-and-white or in color, using regular film. Sometimes in an entire roll of thirty-six exposures, even where several shots are taken of the exact same scene, the people remaining in place, on one or more of the prints there will appear a strange glowing shape, as though a form of static electricity were hovering between the people in the picture. Detailed examination of the conditions under which the film was exposed, processed, and printed and of the camera itself, and then shooting the scene again with a different camera and different film, often reproduces the same results. *Something* is present that makes no sense in our orderly world. It is an energy form of some kind that emits a glow in visible light. Quickly identifying the phenomenon as a "ghost" is simply leaping before a really good look. Put simply, no one *knows* what these energy forms represent. They might well *be* ghosts or they may be electrical or magnetic emanations from the bodies and/or minds of the people who are standing for their pictures to be taken.

On such occasions *the ghosts are us.* The energy output of the human body and brain is astounding, and affects at times strong and sometimes severe physical force on immediate surroundings and objects. With normal vision and within the visible light spectrum, the effects are actually much less visible or noticeable than they are with technological enhancement. Using light-enhancing binoculars and other tools for seeing in near-darkness brings out people and objects with astonishing relief when nothing can be seen with the unaided eye. An incredible world is displayed to the person with light-enhancing equipment, infrared systems, and other devices, while the individual without such help is immersed in a deep gloom within which nothing is visually perceptible.

Sometimes it's not even a matter of technical enhancement, but simply a variation in the visual ability of the observer. Two people standing side by side and looking at precisely the same scene can see entirely different objects before them—if one of the two people is color blind. This was a lesson learned quickly, and used with dramatic effect, in World War II. Photographs taken in color of extremely well-camouflaged installations would often show only what the enemy wished to be shown—hills, fields, trees, shrubbery. To someone with normal vision, that is.

But to the person who was color blind, the camouflage was just about useless! He or she could see right through the colors that so effectively concealed the target buildings. What ensued was a strange reversal of who was sought for military duty. Because colored light signals are often vital to proper communications and identification in military operations, anyone who is color blind was declared "unfit" for military service. Then, abruptly, *not* being able to distinguish colors became of vital import to military intelligence for photographic interpretation.

There is a connection between being able to see a ghost where other people see nothing, and seeing camouflaged buildings where other people see only bland landscapes of trees and shrubbery. It began to make sense out of those situations where only a few people could see a ghostly figure.

This element of seeing is critical in trying to separate what we have always accepted as "natural" and those moments, events, and places where the "natural" is impossible and therefore becomes "supernatural." The latter presents a serious problem, because the very mention of the word *supernatural* leads many investigators and scientists to reject outright anything even associated with that term. They suffer in their own way from the myopia of not understanding this "visualability."

Thousands of hapless people in the world hear voices in their heads. Or, just as likely, the strains of Mozart or the beat of the Beatles resound and echo through their skulls. They are miles from anything that plays music and, without respite from this invasion of their senses, they often believe they are going mad. The truth is they're absolutely normal, they do hear voices and/or music.

Almost every one of us has had dental work done that left metallic fillings in the mouth. That's the receiving antenna and radio! A combination of the metals, the electrical output of the body (the "battery"), and a certain level of sodium and liquids turns some people into perfect receiving systems for radio waves. For years these people believed they were bewitched or were going crazy when actually they were functioning in a perfectly natural manner.

Then there are people who must endure the ringing of "ghost telephones" in their homes (or offices or even cars with cellular phones). This event—the sudden ringing of the telephone *when no one is calling their number*—baffles and often frightens people. Then suddenly their automatic garage door starts grinding its way up to the garage ceiling, starts down again, and sometimes goes up and down in this manner for several minutes. Or lights flash on and off in the home.

If there are remote-control systems for the garage doors, or stereo systems, or the lights, and especially if there is a radiophone in the house, what is bewitching the home is a system of remote control that is set off by airliners or other large aircraft flying overhead that have extremely powerful radio transmitters. Often the frequencies overlap, and a position report becomes the signal to ring the telephone, spring the garage doors, kick in the microwave, or start music blasting from a stereo system.

There are, however, certain people who function as powerful electrical dynamos that wreak havoc for hundreds of feet around their bodies. If we still thought of witches and devils in this age of technology, then it's likely that our society would still be burning people at the stake for these "supernatural powers."

Especially Pauline Shaw, who lives in Cheshire, England.

ELECTRIC WOMAN

In the space of about three years, Pauline Shaw destroyed about fifteen thousand dollars' worth of electrical equipment. Not a bit of it was done deliberately. Indeed, Shaw wished fervently that she could prevent what was happening—because any home she entered as a guest was at once subjected to violent damage to the electrical equipment. If she went into an office building, her path through the building was strewn with destroyed light bulbs, typewriters, computers, and anything else electrical.

Pauline Shaw is a human electrical dynamo. Something happened during her development to make her body become an incredible transmitter of electrical energy. Here is a woman—pretty, pleasant, intelligent, looking perfectly normal—and she destroys toasters, electric irons, washers and dryers, radios and televisions, video recorders, uncounted light bulbs, computers. She has no control over those moments where her body goes ZAP! and all hell breaks loose.

So Oxford University tested her. They were astonished. Consider that your average high-powered microwave oven in your average home cooks with about 700 volts of electricity. *Pauline Shaw's body hurls out an electrical charge of 80,000 volts!*

She was released from her job because the computers in her office and shop tended to go on the fritz without warning, and they did this so often the computers were worthless. Once they sent her packing, the computers (after repairs) worked just fine. Her bank appreciates her doing her business from a long way off—preferably by mail. On one occasion she leaned casually on a computer terminal during a bank visit and seconds later the entire computer system just *died.* Electronic darkness, as it were.

If you meet this charming lady and shake her hand, you may not feel anything but warm pressure. But if her body decides to let loose at that moment, just touching her skin against yours can send you tumbling backward from a powerful electrical shock.

Michael Shallis of Oxford University, recognized as an authority on the unseen forces of the human body, especially its electrical characteristics, is tremendously impressed by Pauline Shaw. It is, if not natural, a rare physiological condition. To Shallis, the condition results from "an abnormal metabolism of a whole range of foods. The breakdown of food products affects the electromagnetic fields found in the body. If any environment static is picked up in addition, strong electrical fields can build up on the skin."

That is an understatement. Pauline Shaw has to live in the past. That is, she can't have electrical appliances within range. So she cooks with gas and lives in a household we might have found before Thomas Edison gave us light bulbs, Marconi gave us radio, and the world entered the age of electricity.

Imagine your home life without electricity. Think of the gas range, the candles, the absence of radio and television and VCR, no ringing of a telephone, and the need to write longhand or use a manual typewriter. . . .

But the point of all this is to illustrate the tremendous energies playing about us—and to emphasize that all of us are constantly emitting forces quite unknown to us *that interact with the forces of other beings.*

Simply try to judge a cup of love, a vial of hate, a spoon of affection, a dollop of honesty, a bucket of friendship, or a glass of pain and misery. You might try a box of sensuality or even define the fragrance of romance, or capture in a bottle a measure of grief. Ah, an ounce of hope? What?

These are all the invisible, irreproducible, immeasurable, impossible-to-prove elements that govern our lives, and you cannot put any of them in a bottle or under the microscope.

HOW REAL THE DREAM?

September 29, 1961, is a date several pilots, a representative of Columbia Pictures, and an official of Metro Media news productions of New York will remember all their lives.

This story begins with the decision of Columbia Pictures of Hollywood and their associates in England to make a film of the novel *The War Lover*. To shoot the film in England, where the original World War II action took place, it was necessary to find, bring back to flyable condition, and then ferry to England three Boeing B-17 Flying Fortress bombers, which would then be painted in wartime colors to fulfill their roles in the film.

The three Fortresses, with an American, Australian, and English crew, had flown to the northeast after a series of misadventures in the flight across the United States. Now they were set to depart from Teterboro Airport in New Jersey, ready for the hop to Boston, where they would remain overnight, and the next day go on to Gander, Newfoundland, in Canada.

Before takeoff, Bert Perlmutter, a man living in Plainview, Long Island, learned that a close friend of his was one of the pilots for the B-17 adventure. During World War II Perlmutter had been a flight engineer and top turret gunner in a Flying Fortress on many missions over Germany.

Sixteen years had passed since the war's end. Perlmutter was anxious to impart to his teenaged daughter what it was *really* like inside a B-17 in flight. This might be the only chance he would ever have. He called his pilot friend with a request.

"Let me fly with you guys up to Boston. I want to bring my daughter, let her live for a little while what it was like, hear the sounds, feel the motions. Let her taste a bit of the history of her old man."

The pilots gave their nod, and Perlmutter and his daughter arrived a few hours later in Teterboro Airport. Twenty minutes later the formation was airborne and on its way to Boston. It was a beautiful flight, excellent flying conditions, with a wide-open sky. The fuselage of the airplane carrying Perlmutter and his daughter was crammed with spare parts, machine guns, and long belts of .50-caliber ammunition with all the rounds drilled to render them harmless. To find a place to sit or stretch out in the fuselage meant sprawling on all the equipment or lying down on one of the two folding cots that swung down from the inside walls.

The Fortress rocked and bounced gently as it droned smoothly, all four engines and propellers throbbing in unison. It wasn't long before the gentle motions and the warmth of the sun's rays slanting through the gunners' windows worked like a sleeping potion for the young girl. She stretched out on one cot. On the other side, Bert Perlmutter was lost in deep thought. The crewmen knew that memories were hammering through this man's mind. In an airplane exactly like this one he had risked death time and again as German fighters swarmed in, and the gunners met their fire with hammering bursts of their own heavy machine guns. Men had bled and died in planes just like this very Fortress, and in his mind Perlmutter was back in Germany, reliving that life. As he fell asleep Perlmutter's face twitched as a painful memory darted through his mind now and again.

Four men sat in the fuselage: two pilots and the navigator and radioman up front in the flight deck. The four men sat on crates and a huge tire, relaxed, smoking. Looking back from their position, the interior of the bomber had a mystic quality, the result of dust bouncing from aircraft motion and the slanting rays of the sun.

Then one man gasped. His face seemed to freeze as he stared back through the Fortress. "Holy . . ." Words failed him, but the look on his face brought the others to follow his gaze. Another pilot said, slowly and deliberately, "I don't believe . . . hey, you guys, am I really seeing what I think I'm seeing?"

Four men looked, four men shared the same sight. They watched a dream of years gone by taking shape before them.

Bert Perlmutter, now deep into sleep and dreaming, twitched on the cot. His mouth worked with words spoken only in his mind. Perspiration gleamed on his face. Sometimes he seemed to be shouting or screaming. At other times he appeared to be struggling physically.

But what the four men witnessed seemed impossible. Perlmutter's own view of sixteen or seventeen years before *was taking form before their eyes.* In that ethereal light in the swaying Fortress, as if through shimmering gauze, they saw dim shadows moving. Two men in heavy flight suits, wearing oxygen masks, gripped .50-caliber machine guns in the waist position. They were calling out to one another, the guns visibly hammering, shell casings flying through the air. Not a sound emerged as the four astonished men watched the ghostly tableau of a battle raging 25,000 feet over wartime Germany. Then one man lurched and moved with great effort toward the stunned pilots, his face concealed within his leather helmet, goggles, and oxygen mask. The watchers saw that one of his hands had been blown away, leaving only a bloody stump where the wrist ended.

The other man half-dragged him to the open space of the navigator's upward-firing gun position. They watched the man in the mask heave his friend upward and shove the blood-spurting arm into the screaming windblast. Five miles high the temperature would have been about forty degrees below zero. The terrible cold closed off the ghastly wound, freezing blood and flesh. Then there was a gasp as Bert Perlmutter awakened, sitting upright, soaked in sweat.

The ghostly figures were gone. Bert's daughter slept quietly. One pilot lit a cigarette for Bert; he took it with shaking hands.

That night the four witnesses to the ghostly figures in the B-17 fuselage finally faced one another. "Who was the guy in the mask and goggles?"

"That was Bert Perlmutter," a pilot answered.

"But how could we see what we did! And we *all* saw those gunners, over Germany, way back when . . ."

"Yeah, I know," the older pilot told his friends. "You see, I've known Perlmutter a long time. He was a flight engineer and top turret gunner on his Fortress. On the raid against Schweinfurt in October of 1943, the one they call Black Thursday, one of Bert's gunners had his hand blown off. Bert dragged him to that top gun position and shoved his stump into the wind to freeze it. He saved the man's life."

"That's what we saw today, then. . . ."

"Yeah."

"How could *we* see what Bert was dreaming? I mean, that's a materialization of a dream! Like going back in time!"

"That's what Bert did. Somehow, it was so intense he projected to us. I guess. Anyway, we shared it with him."

One pilot showed his discomfort. "Anybody like to explain to me how it ended the way it did?"

The discomfort was almost physical. Hard whiskey went down like water with no effect—because of one last thing that had happened in the Fortress.

Just before Bert woke his daughter, something on the bomber's floor caught his eye. The pilots watched him lean down and pick up something that glinted in the sun. He held it up.

It was the round for a .50-caliber machine gun. Shiny,

brand-new, just like it was in 1943. *There wasn't any hole drilled in the round.* It was a hot round—never fired. And it wasn't in the airplane when it took off from Teterboro.

Bert had turned it around and around. He had shaken his head slowly and placed the machine-gun round in his pocket, then gently awakened his daughter. They had sat tightly together as the Fortress sighed back to earth and landed gently.

TIMESLIP

Imagine you can transport yourself back to an event involving hundreds of men—with witnesses too many to count. You find yourself climbing a nasty ridgeline perhaps thirty miles north of Oxford, a place called Edgehill, and the chill of winter settles in for the night. It is October 23, 1642, and in the morning the battle will rage between the fielded army of King Charles I and the gathered forces of Robert Devereax, the third Earl of Essex.

The two forces clashed shortly after dawn. Why remember the battle of Edgehill? As military engagements go it was particularly savage. No great events occurred to be remembered with unusual praise or honor. Men fired pistols at point-blank range, and when their gunpowder was gone they hacked and slashed at one another in senseless butchering of limbs and bodies. They fought all day, weary to the bone, staggering about, killing aimlessly and listlessly, and by nightfall their greatest desire was to separate, the survivors wanting no more than to be out of sword range. In darkness they collected their wounded, gathered fallen weapons, crossed paths with enemies—but fought no more. They were exhausted and desperate for rest and sleep. Edgehill was nothing, a pile of hilly scrub not worth a single shot, but now it was bloody and flecked with the remains of bodies.

By morning they were ready to resume, but instead, each side gathered its wounded and its weapons and, in some semblance of soldierly pride, forced themselves into marching order and gratefully left the grounds of battle.

And there Edgehill should have passed into history. There should have been no more than perhaps a single reference to an unnecessary battle, fought stupidly if bloodily, with nothing gained save the spilling of blood and hacking of bodies.

Quiet returned to Edgehill, the battles moved elsewhere, and it *seemed* to be sliding into the past.

Several months later, as elaborately prepared records attest, the silence of Edgehill was broken with faint sounds, with the call of horns and then the ghostly rattle of drums signaling armed men into position to do battle. Along a roadway that passed by and beneath the scrub hillocks of Edgehill, several passersby brought their carriages to a stop. They heard unusual sounds where nothing should have been.

The sounds grew louder. The drumrolls became absolutely frightening. The battle was beginning again between the two armies, *but it was taking place in the sky.*

Let the record tell it as it was written down in 1643 by a historian of that time, who in good faith and amazement put the astonishing events to paper; he called it "A Great Wonder in Heaven."

> It came that the travelers, astonished and fearful, beheld in the air the same incorporeal soldiers that made these clamours . . . and one army was of the King's colours, and the other carrying those of the Parliament's at their head. The struggle lasted till two or three in the morning . . . continued this dreadful fight, the clattering of arms, noises of cannon, cries of soldiers . . . amazing and terrifying the poor men on the road who saw all this at the doorstep to the heavens.

Those on the roadway rushed to the nearest town to relate breathlessly what they had seen and heard, and how the flailing armies and uproar finally faded from sight and sound. They were suspected of being either drunk or mad, so the night following, the town's leaders and officials joined with those who had been on the road the night before.

It happened again, the booming of cannon, shrieks of dying men, screaming of horses, the drumrolls, all of it. Shocked and frightened officials immediately rushed to the King and related the events. King Charles was not one to question so many loyal subjects, but to play safely on the side of sanity and reality, he dispatched a group of his officers to Edgehill, telling them to be sharp in their observations so that the Crown might be able to dismiss this nonsense once and for all.

For the third night in a row the armies joined in the sky and the hills shook to the hammering blows and sounds of the battle. It went further than that, as the officers reported back to the King. Not only had they seen and heard the struggle—*but they had recognized close friends with whom they had fought side by side and whom they had seen die from gunshot and sword wounds.*

Somehow, in a way yet unknown to us, the veils closed and silence returned to the skies of Edgehill.

9
PROPHECY FOR APOLLO

It is 1970. Along the middle-eastern coast of Florida, tension is high. Excitement buzzes day and night, emphasized during the evening hours by great beams of light stabbing crisscross into the heavens over the Kennedy Space Center. The nation and the world focus their attention on one specific point of land overlooking the Atlantic Ocean. This is Pad 39A—an inadequate name for this monster temple of steel, cabling, massive blocks of reinforced concrete, huge ribbed tunnels of metal, high thick towers, and steel pins wider than the body of a man. On that pad stands a rocket as tall as a forty-story building. Atop the 3,200 tons of the most powerful rocket ever built is a cone-shaped vehicle in which three men will ride this monster away from Earth.

This is *Apollo 13*, humankind's third attempt to land two astronauts on the surface of the moon. Their steed is the enormous *Saturn V*, containing a volatile mixture of enough chemicals that, if this monster ever exploded on its launch pad, it would hurl out a blast equal to that from a small atomic bomb. Three men will wager their lives that all will go well.

There is doubt, of course. There is always doubt when you mix liquid oxygen, liquid hydrogen, and other chemicals and dozens of engines large and small, and you gamble that this machine will hurl its cargo of life away from our world at the speed of 25,000 miles an hour—*seven miles every second*. At such a stupendous velocity, even the failure of a small part can blossom into a fiery, shattering explosion.

There is also doubt elsewhere. This doubt rises from puzzlement, but it is not on the broad expanse of the launch pad on Merritt Island. It is south some fifty miles in a house on Riverside Avenue along the edge of the Indian River in the town of Melbourne Beach. This is the home and writing studio of Dame Sybil Leek. She is the author of nearly fifty books. She has also published thousands of newspaper columns and magazine articles. Her advice is sought by people throughout the world. She is also a qualified authority on antiques. She has owned restaurants and she owns and operates private schools, and not far from her home and studio is her Trans-Atlantic Art Gallery located in the posh Warwick Hotel.

She is also a world-renowned astrologer.

And she is a witch.

Many people know *who* she is but those who know the person make up a closed and tight circle, for she limits those with whom she shares her innermost thoughts. Yet to one and all she is a most impressive individual. She is fascinating, entertaining, erudite, mysterious, inviting, and even a formidable and at times frightening individual.

But—*a witch?*

Believe it. Millions of people know Dame Sybil Leek as the White Witch of England. She represents many others who are members of a religious group that has existed for centuries. A witch can be many things to many people, but Dame Sybil answers to none of the judgments.

"Astrology is my science," Dame Sybil declared, "witchcraft is my religion, and writing is my profession."

What was the connection between Dame Sybil Leek in Melbourne Beach and just northward along the Florida coast, the giant standing poised to hurl three men to another world a quarter of a million miles from Earth?

The history of the Apollo program has been written, catalogued, detailed, and recorded with millions of words and tens of thousands of photographs as well as video and film. These make up the hardware, the epic moments, and the thrill and the danger. But that's the outside cover of the

book of Apollo, and it is scarce in its most personal
moments.

Dame Sybil Leek was a pivotal flash point in that
history. The wives and families of the astronauts endured
the dangers in their own way. It can be a frightening, even
terrifying sight to watch your loved one atop a shrieking,
bellowing fire monster of gargantuan proportion. If a fuel
line ruptures or a computer balks or a solenoid fails, well,
there are only so many exits.

The best that NASA could tell the astronauts' wives
was simply not enough. The most encouraging words
failed to convey a sense of security. These women were
frightened, aghast with the reality of it all, and the smiling
faces they conveyed to the public—the expressions of confidence—that was for show.

Inside, they wanted more. They wanted to know as
much as possible about what *might* happen to their loved
ones.

So wives, families, friends turned to Dame Sybil Leek
and asked for what she could see in the future. They asked
her to consult whatever celestial bodies were necessary to
find the critical junctures to supply the information that
would tell them what might, what could, what *would*
happen.

Here, on the coast next to the great spaceport that led
to other worlds, they cast aside the science and the technology and the computers, the engineering and the creativ-
ity, and they turned to one woman and her astrological
skills to create horoscopes for them.

Not that they did so openly. To consult an astrologer
was to flaunt science and to exhibit a complete lack of
faith in the space program. That would be bad publicity
and grist for the gossip mill. So many of the visits, the
meetings, the information these people sought was kept
under the strictest confidence by everyone concerned. But
not all—some family members were so concerned about
the welfare of their loved ones that they didn't give a damn
what NASA or anyone else thought of what they did. They

went openly to Sybil Leek and said to hell with the critics.

It was shortly before *Apollo 13* was scheduled to depart this blue and lovely planet to journey to a cratered, barren, dusty slagheap of a moon a quarter of a million miles across an ocean of vacuum and hard radiation. Dame Sybil had done this before. Projects Mercury and Gemini had lofted astronauts into Earth orbit, and there were moments of enormous tension and near-disaster all the way through those programs. And then came Apollo, huge, dwarfing what had gone before, incredibly more intricate and demanding in both performance and reliability. Dame Sybil faced a complexity of astrological problems.

The night came when Dame Sybil was working with great frustration on her astrological forecast for *Apollo 13*. On this night, in Melbourne Beach, on the edge of the ocean, Sybil was troubled by this upcoming event. More than troubled. She had dark thoughts; unease stalked her home studio. It was strange for her to feel this way, for she was no outsider to this world of science, flight, and space.

Sybil Leek had flown in everything from small single-engined airplanes to clattering helicopters to huge jets spanning the globe. She knew engineering, rocketry, and celestial mechanics. She was, in short, *knowledgeable*.

Yet this troubling of spirit as she worked on *Apollo 13* persisted. At three o'clock in the morning, Sybil ran hard up against the wall bedeviling her progress. It was an unknown, something she could not quite compute in her horoscope preparations for the three astronauts.

Dame Sybil and her son Julian, a photographer, newsman, and working associate with Sybil, had spread papers and charts and diagrams and references from the living room into the bedroom. Notes and computations spread across the bed and onto the floor beyond. The air was charged with frustration, which only drove Dame Sybil to work with unusual fervor.

Soon the papers and charts spread farther throughout the house, into the kitchen and on tables and chairs, a great semicircle of paperwork from studio to bedroom to kitchen and beyond. And still what she sought to solve eluded her.

Then the first clues began to emerge. There were hints of incompatibility involving the three men. There was a reference point in her work that pointed to nonsuccess, data to terrify the astronauts' families. Sybil mulled over her work. The two previous landings on the moon, *Apollo 11* and *Apollo 12*, were completely different from what she saw emerging in the patterns for *Apollo 13*. She saw signs of grave danger, a hovering shadowy presence, possibly death, for at least two of the three astronauts.

There was the flaw. Two out of three. Two astronauts were in grave danger. *The third was not!*

Sybil knew the schedules and flight information for the Apollo missions. At first glance there was a simple answer to why two astronauts could be so threatened while the third was free of the danger signs. When the *Apollo* flamed into orbit about the moon, and preparations were complete to land, two men in the Lunar Module were to break away from the heavy Command Module and Service Module. The latter would remain in lunar orbit, really quite safe in that gravity slot, while the two astronauts in the landing ship would go through elaborate powered maneuvers and work their way down to a landing, balancing on rocket flame, on a world where there is no atmosphere.

Obviously the two astronauts powering for the surface landing were taking risks much greater than the one waiting for them in the Command Module orbiting the moon.

But the elation at working out the specifics faded quickly. "That's *not* it," Sybil snapped aloud. "Every launching is filled with dangers. That rocket lifts off with the power of twenty Hoover Dams. Dozens of engines of all sizes burn through the ascent. But one of those men isn't in danger of *any* kind, and he's scheduled to ride that fire mountain all the way to the moon, to say nothing of the return trip when they smash into Earth's atmosphere at twenty-five thousand miles an hour! There is danger there for everyone, except . . . except that one man is free of that danger. It does not fit!"

Sybil yielded to the immovable. She prepared her findings, and the problems, in meticulous detail. She put in *everything*, emphasizing her prediction of danger for two, none for one. She sent a registered-mail copy to Dr. Rudy Wells in Cocoa Beach, a former Air Force flight surgeon. She sent one to herself, several more went out to other people, and one was locked in a bank vault. Now she was committed to her prediction. There was absolutely no way to alter in any way what she had committed to paper and registered mail, no matter how unrealistic it all appeared to be.

Sybil Leek and her sons, Julian and Stephen, were with the press at the spaceport to watch *Apollo 13* blast off. *But there had been a change in the mission plans for* Apollo 13. . . .

Just a few days before scheduled lift-off, one of the three astronauts had been exposed to a youngster with a sudden disease, common enough for children, but potentially deadly to an adult. NASA had no choice—they immediately removed the astronaut from the crew and brought in the standby.

The rest is history. Dame Sybil Leek's astrological forecast was incredibly accurate. "*Two of the astronauts are in grave danger. But not the third man.*" Of course! The third man was removed from the mission *before* launch.

And this was the mission on which the Apollo program came the closest to losing the entire crew. While *Apollo 13* was en route to the moon, the Service Module exploded. Within minutes the danger was extreme. Life-giving oxygen, power, and other elements critical to survival were ejected into space. A combination of courage, skill in space, and a superb mission control team on Earth all combined to extricate the astronauts from what appeared, for a time, to be certain death.

Had the explosion taken place closer to the moon, or anywhere else on the mission profile except where it did, the odds against survival would have been even higher. But only *two* of those men in the charts Sybil Leek prepared that moody night were ever in danger.

Dame Sybil's notes, registered and sealed long before the flight, matched the technical events that finally transpired with incredible precision. There were many discussions of how Dame Sybil could have known the odds for and against the crew of *Apollo 13*. Few NASA officials believe in horoscopes or in astrological forecasts. Astrology breaks every rule of science and technology known. Yet they admit they were stunned by the accuracy of Dame Sybil Leek's predictions. To them it could not be what they would call a "natural" event.

Does this make it *supernatural*?

10
THAT DAMNED TRAPEZIUM

A private yacht departs from a marina on the east coast of Florida on its way to Bermuda. The weather is perfect: scattered clouds, light winds, a calm sea. Two days later the weather conditions have remained much the same, but all contact with the vessel is lost. It no longer transmits radio signals and it fails to respond to radioed queries from the U.S. Coast Guard or any other maritime agency. There is as yet little cause for alarm, but days go by and soon the ship is overdue in Bermuda. After another day or two a search begins. All ships in the area are alerted to be on the lookout for the missing yacht or for any signs of debris. The same message is sent to aircraft flying through the area, but when there is still nothing to be found a major and deliberate search is set in motion, including the use of ocean-monitoring satellites, and military reconnaissance aircraft that can detect even a rowboat on the high seas.

Nothing. The yacht has disappeared. The yacht's loss must go on the record books attributed to "reasons unknown." There is nothing else to go by. There are probabilities and possibilities. There could have been an explosion in the engine room, setting off the fuel tanks in a disastrous fiery blast that prevented any emergency signals from being broadcast. The yacht could have been waylaid by heavily armed pirate ships, an activity in today's world that receives little publicity but is an ongoing danger. A rogue wave may have swamped the ship without warning. Or a neutercane—a freak meteorological event that appears as a confined and violent storm with winds exceeding 120 miles per hour, huge waves, barrages of lightning, and waterspouts—may have torn open the ship and sent it to the bottom.

Whatever the cause, the yacht is gone without a trace. To the statisticians, it is one more mystery of the area that has become infamous as the Bermuda Triangle. To the family and friends of the people lost with the yacht, it is a horrible disaster, made all the worse by not knowing what really happened.

Much the same pattern has attended the loss of hundreds of aircraft, from small single-engined planes to huge four-engined airliners and military bombers, ranging from low altitude to ten miles above the ocean surface. Freak weather conditions, such as lightning strikes in a cloudless sky, have been witnessed in the Triangle. Sudden storms spring up. Airplanes have exploded without warning when their fuel tanks ignited. Dozens of ambiguous events ram ships beneath the ocean and swat airplanes from the sky without warning of any kind. Inexplicable messages have been received from both aircraft and ships with pilots and navigators shouting about some unidentified but terrible danger—followed by a silence that has never been explained.

The Bermuda Triangle is a great swath of the Atlantic Ocean that takes a devastating toll of ships and aircraft. Even when all the natural possibilities have been exhausted, the number of ships and planes lost forever, often without any evidence of any kind, is so great that anyone familiar with the oceans or with flight has to believe that some incredible mystery lies behind these tragedies. It has also been called the Devil's Triangle, the Devil's Graveyard, the Devil's Sea, the Triangle of the Damned, and other colorful names. Attempting to describe a specific area of the Atlantic Ocean has brought on its own curse.

What is maddening to the serious researcher is that so many of the mysterious disappearances and strange events encountered in this area of ocean are absolutely real and confirmed. The reports of skilled veteran observers have established, if not a pattern, at least identifiable forces and their impact on ships and aircraft.

In short, things happen in the Bermuda Triangle that, once again, skeptics and scientists attribute to "normal forces and events." Scientists, let alone skeptics, still cannot identify the sources of the problems or the manner in which ships and aircraft have either been struck down, destroyed, or bedeviled by strange forces. How do we know that such forces exist?

Many of the ships and aircraft have survived their encounters. Therefore researchers have been able to accumulate and categorize times, places, and just what did take place. They have arrived at hard and meaningful conclusions. They do not always produce answers, but they do establish the reality of the occurrences.

In the thirty years from 1945 through 1975, 67 ships and boats of all sizes, and at least 192 aircraft of all types, involving approximately 1,700 human beings vanished within the Bermuda Triangle, the vast majority of them leaving not a shred of evidence to make it clear what happened.

As convenient as it may be to define the "Triangle" by stabbing a pencil on the chart dot marked Bermuda and proceeding from that point, that's being specific without justification. Take Bermuda and its surrounding waters, perhaps two hundred miles in all directions, and then draw a wide band westward to Wilmington/North Myrtle Beach on the U.S. mainland. From this area, which sometimes extends inland, make another wide swath generally southward, but taking in the entire coastline down to approximately a hundred miles south of Key West. Continue southeast, still with that wide swath, to Puerto Rico (the area of the island and surrounding waters), and then bend around in a generally northeast direction back to Bermuda. Now we have a rectangle with four unequal sides, or a trapezium, not really a triangle.

The 67 ships and 192 aircraft *confirmed lost* in the

Triangle do not constitute the actual number of ships and planes lost in the thirty years from 1945 to 1975. There have also been countless unconfirmed, inconclusive losses. Consider the many high-security military missions involved. If the United States is carrying out combat maneuvers under high security and an experimental aircraft is lost, explanations or comments from the sources that control the release of such data are simply not going to appear. This happens all the time. Should we lose an *Aurora* advanced reconnaissance flight system, which first augmented and then replaced the Lockheed SR-71 Blackbird triple-supersonic aircraft, everything will be done to keep that information from release—especially if the *Aurora* encountered a totally unexplained phenomenon.

There are less esoteric situations that are even more likely to increase the numbers of the lost. Commercial aircraft, that vanish with several hundred passengers aboard are newsmakers. After all, the aircraft is part of a major fleet, owned by a huge company, is listed in computers and printed schedules, and many other hundreds of people are concerned. When one of these machines vanishes, there's obviously a tumultuous hue and cry.

Not so for many privately owned aircraft, traveling up and down the eastern coastline of the United States or moving through the Bahamas and other islands, that fly through that "chart swath" to Puerto Rico before bending northeast back to Bermuda. Most of these are flown by pilots who hew to the regulations and file necessary flight plans, but not all. Pilots often fly into this area without filing a flight plan, which leaves behind a record of names and addresses, and the type and number of the aircraft. And sometimes the flight plan itself may be a ruse—meant to mislead authorities so that the pilot can disappear from sight, for the time needed to complete some illegal or immoral act. Government records show that thousands of drug-running and people-smuggling flights take place every year. And then there are other pilots who simply get caught up in weather and end up accidently in the Triangle.

Thousands of sea voyages are also made through the Triangle in complete safety. Tens of thousands of aircraft flights traverse the Triangle without a hint of trouble. These facts are as important as any other.

Perhaps the only meaningful way of knowing some of the perils of the Triangle comes from people who have survived conditions and effects that meteorologists and scientists insist cannot exist. This provides detailed, first-hand knowledge of the forces that affect ships and planes and *almost* take them down.

The greater the skill, experience, and knowledge of the person or persons involved, obviously the more reliable the details related about a near-loss while traversing the Triangle. One incident that happened some years ago is considered a classic. The nature of what happened, and how it happened, and the extraordinary skills and experience of the pilot involved—a story this man kept secret for many years, in fact, until shortly before his death—deserves special attention.

LOST!

The pilot left Havana, Cuba, at 1:35 A.M. on a long, planned flight that would take him directly to Saint Louis, Missouri. He planned to cross the Straits of Florida and then continue on in his single-engined plane to his destination. Most of his flying would be by dead reckoning—he had to be expert at his business. This was 1928, and the superb electronic navigation aids pilots enjoy today were unheard of in those times. But *this* pilot was not only experienced, he was judged one of the best in the world.

And in 1928 no one had ever even heard of any area called the Bermuda Triangle.

As the pilot left Cuba behind and flew over open water, strange things began to happen inside the cabin, and then to the plane. He watched his magnetic compass start to turn to the right, slow down, stop, and then immediately begin a turn to the left, right again, left again, and suddenly it was rotating around and around. The rotational movement increased until it was a blur.

It wasn't supposed to do that. In fact, in flight over the ocean, such a thing was supposed to be impossible. A magnetic compass can be affected to indicate an "off" reading, but they just do not spin madly about. The pilot recalled that every now and then some flier somewhere would talk about his magnetic compass "going wild" or "berserk" and spinning so fast it would even break its container bowl and splash alcohol over the instrument panel. That was practically happening now.

This particular aircraft also had an earth induction indicator, a solid piece of navigation equipment. It could be used for crossing oceans. Many pilots used them religiously for reliable long-range navigation. But now the EII in this plane went completely bananas. First it twitched from side to side, then it jerked a bit more wildly, and finally it wandered erratically, pointing first one way, then another, indicating a course that made no sense.

The pilot was aware that something very extraordinary was happening. He had little idea what it might be—some incredible magnetic field, or electromagnetic vortex, or localized whirlpool of energy. He had to fly this airplane at night over a very big ocean and he didn't know what direction he was flying.

Now both compasses were useless. The pilot had no way to use those instruments for guidance, to check his heading or his course, or to even revert back to dead reckoning to determine his course and changing position.

But he was a good pilot. He kept flying as steadily as he could, using star references to hold course. That worked perfectly until a strange mist, unlike anything he'd ever encountered before, that had not been forecast by the weather crews for this flight, settled through the entire area. This was not fog as he had ever known it, hugging the ground or the ocean surface. This fog was everywhere. It completely blinded the pilot. Above the pilot the stars were so dim they were useless for navigation.

The pilot eased his plane into a steady descent. He decided to fly as low as possible—in the dark. What he hoped to do, what he had done before elsewhere, was to fly so low he'd be able to pick out whitecaps on the ocean surface and then determine their size and direction. That would provide him with at least a rough idea of the wind direction, its force, and if it had changed from the original forecasts.

The plan failed. The air became turbulent, the mist thicker, and because there was no critical danger of smashing into the sea, he eased back on the stick into a steady, gentle climb.

All he could do now was try to hold the airplane as steady as possible using his experience, his senses, and his intelligence—to forge what he hoped was straight ahead until the insane weather might disappear and the whirling compasses return to normal functioning.

He kept flying. The minutes passed like wet sand stuck in the narrow neck of an hourglass. Then, finally, dawn began to streak the eastern horizon. Now he had his first definite clue as to direction. All he needed to do was to fly into the darkest part of the sky and he knew he'd be heading west.

But he'd never seen a dawn quite like this one. He found it difficult to accept what the sky was showing him. Later he would describe this as flying through "dark milk."

Night yielded to the rising sun as it flooded the "dark milk" of the skies. With every moment of brightening, visibility improved. There below him—finally—he could see the surface of the earth. He saw he was on a coastline and still flying westward. He was startled and pleased as he watched the spinning magnetic compass begin to slow and then settle down and indicate the magnetic headings perfectly. He shifted his gaze to the earth induction compass that had behaved like a light bush in a high wind. It was as steady as a rock.

Yet for a while the pilot could not determine his exact location. He kept scanning the shoreline, trying to identify features he might recognize. No luck. He placed his flight chart before him. Still . . . nothing. Where was he? He looked at another chart and the lines on the paper matched those of the shoreline below. He shook his head in wonder. If what he saw was true, then he was off course. Far off course. So far off course that he could never have reached this position in the hours of the night with the amount of fuel he had on board.

Nothing fit. Nothing made any sense, not the entire night, the spinning compasses, the haze that had enveloped him and blocked him from the world, or that sensation of a sky turned to "dark milk" until the murky heavy mists were banished by the sun.

He had never known anything like it. It lay beyond his understanding of the skies, and he was a master aviator. Nothing he knew of this world could make possible what he had lived through this night. Never had he been so lost as he was this morning until the charts finally matched the contours of the shoreline.

In everything he ever subsequently said or wrote about his career, he refrained from bringing attention to this flight. This man, known throughout the world and revered by millions, kept his silence gripped tightly to himself. Finally he wrote his last book, published in 1976, where at long last he revealed what had happened.

He did not believe he would be believed. He believed in the possible; what had happened, by all the laws of flight and physics he knew, simply could not be. Something far beyond his ken had happened. Something . . . strange.

And yet, most pilots accept that he would have been believed. Because who would doubt the man who was flying from Cuba to Saint Louis in the *Spirit of Saint Louis*?

Charles Lindbergh.

JUNE 11, 1986

The aircraft is a Consolidated PBY-6A Catalina, first flown in 1935, so at the time of this flight the design is better than fifty years old. It is a great machine with the hull of a boat and the wings and tail of an airplane. It carried passengers as a commercial airliner in the 1930s through the Pacific and to remote areas of the world. It performed yeoman service before, during, and after World War II. But the wars are far behind for the Catalina, and this particular PBY is the personal aircraft of Connie Edwards of Big Spring, Texas.

In May 1986 the Catalina left Texas to begin a long-range flight across the United States to Canada. It then flew to the Azores in the Atlantic, on to Lisbon, Portugal, then to Santiago, Spain, to a landing in Plymouth Harbor in England, and on to Yeovilton in England. Its return flight brought it from Yeovilton back to Lajes in the Azores, and then to a long flight to Bermuda. Now, on June 11, 1986, the Catalina is ready for the leg from Bermuda to JAX (Jacksonville Naval Air Station in northeast Florida).

Aboard the Catalina are some of the most experienced and able pilots in the world. These include Connie Edwards, who has been flying transports, fighters, bombers, and airliners since his teens. Randy Sohn is a jetliner captain with Northwest Airlines, and is qualified by the U.S. government to fly any piston-engined aircraft of any type anywhere in the world. Captain Art Ward has long been one of the leading pilots in the U.S. Navy and is considered by his peers to be the finest instrument pilot and instructor in the business. Al Brown, flight engineer and pilot for the Catalina, is an air force veteran and a master pilot. There is also Major General Malcolm Ryan, also judged by his peers in the Air Force as "one of the greatest test pilots and combat leaders this country has ever had."

The PBY is equipped with the latest instrumentation and avionics (flight electronics) ever developed. There are radar altimeters, HF radios, VLF Omegas for navigation, lorans, ADFs, encoding altimeters, radar altimeters, and an electronics system that can print out photographic maps of the area where the plane will be flying—taken from weather satellites orbiting the Earth. If the airplane was so much as a tenth of a mile off course the pilots became aware of their position immediately. Edwards had two huge fuel tanks slung beneath the wings for more than thirty-two hours of nonstop flight if necessary, and Brown had upgraded the engines for extra power.

When the PBY departed from Bermuda it was into perfect flying weather—what pilots call "severe clear." The satellite photos showed that the nearest clouds along the route were at least two-hundred miles distant.

The flight went beautifully; the PBY flies like a gentle whale, slow and steady and reliable. Then, several hours after takeoff, it happened.

One moment the pilots could see "forever." Suddenly, without a bump or a tremor or any indication that things were different, the outside world was gone. Nothing had changed except that the airplane now "was flying through a huge mass of yellow eggnog."

The wingspan of the PBY from tip to tip is 110 feet, or slightly less than fifty feet from the cockpit to either wing-tip. *From the cockpit the pilots could no longer see either wingtip.* There weren't any clouds or turbulence or anything different except that the PBY, still flying smoothly, seemed completely isolated from the rest of the world. Looking back from the cockpit they could see the long fuselage and the gun blisters on each side. Beyond that— all-encompassing yellow. No sky, no ocean, just that impossible yellow.

Looking forward, the nose was clear, as was the cleat atop the nose for mooring. Beyond the cleat—a universe of thick yellow. Now the pilots were flying strictly by the instruments on the panel before them, balancing airspeed, rate of climb, heading, and altitude.

Everybody remained calm. As crazy as this yellow limbo was, the airplane was flying perfectly well. And since there wasn't anything else to do except *fly*, this is just what they did, even if the world seemed to have disappeared.

Then a new problem arose that couldn't be ignored. The magnetic compass began to swing back and forth in an erratic movement. Abruptly it whipped into a spinning motion that made it useless. The only thing that could cause this effect was some sort of powerful electromagnetic field that had suddenly enveloped the airplane.

That was the first sign that the Catalina was moving through a force field of some unknown origin. Other indications followed like dominoes. The super-advanced electronic systems began to fail as though in the grip of some paralyzing force.

The magnetic compass had been first to go. Gyroscopic instruments followed. The directional gyro (DG), for accurate headings, began a slow revolving motion and followed the mag compass in a steady spin. At about the same time a vital gyro instrument, the artificial horizon, which lets a pilot know the attitude of the airplane (climbing, descending, turning) tumbled over like a dying animal.

The electronics maintained power though their readings stopped making sense. The loran, for long-range navigation, gave idiot readings. Even the electronic gauges that showed remaining quantity and flow rate of fuel blinked on and off and the numbers flickered uselessly up and down. The other gauges with glowing numbers all read 8888888—useless. Then even the radios went brain-dead. They had full power but the PBY couldn't receive any incoming transmissions and there was no way to tell if outgoing transmissions were reaching anyone. All power flow was normal but nothing worked.

Now the pilots were flying by the oldest navigation methods in the world—using barometric pressure readings for speed, altitude, descent or climb, and turning. This demanded absolute attention and skill, because the pilots were flying blind. For a heading there was only one thing to do—fly steadily to where the yellow murk was the brightest, which meant the late afternoon sun.

This went on for several hours. Then, ninety minutes out of JAX (as the records later showed), the yellow limbo vanished. It was as if a switch had clicked. One instant the airplane was in thick murk; in the blink of an eye, as if flying through a curtain, the sky became absolutely clear and visibility was perfect.

Moments later the magnetic and gyro compasses and horizon settled down, and the electronics started functioning as though nothing had ever been wrong with them. Radio contact was established with JAX, the navigational equipment worked perfectly, and the flight continued uneventfully to a smooth landing at the naval air station.

Did these pilots ever learn what this "isolation visually and electronically" from the rest of the world was?

No one has a clue.

NO ANSWER

The enveloping mists and murky yellow sky encountered in the flights of Charles Lindbergh and the Catalina flying boat are by no means isolated incidents. Dozens of pilots who have encountered and survived these mysterious conditions have reported the same effects, something escaping by a much narrower margin.

John Hawke was one such pilot. Hawke was the former lead aerobatic instructor for the Royal Air Force. He was a "natural" pilot who could fly anything with wings. He had made literally hundreds of ocean crossings, flying above the Atlantic, Pacific, and Indian Oceans in everything from small single-engined planes to huge four-engined jetliners.

Yet he came close to disaster on a flight in a twin-engined Piper Aztec from Fort Lauderdale, Florida, to Bermuda. For Hawke this was strictly a "piece of cake" delivery flight. Once at his cruising altitude, he turned on his automatic pilot and sat back to let the miles and hours while away.

Then Hawke's finely honed instincts brought him upright in his seat. The horizon had blurred and seemed to thicken before his eyes into a pasty yellow. He checked and rechecked his instruments; everything seemed fine until he noticed his magnetic compass whipping back and forth and abruptly snapping into a steady whirling motion. But the automatic pilot was flying the airplane perfectly.

Hawke soon discovered he could not remain alert for long. "I felt dizzy. Maybe woozy is a better word, but my balance was slipping away. It was quite like the onset of vertigo, but now my peripheral vision began to darken. Again it was a strange sensation. I'm accustomed to greyouts, when high g-forces begin to dim your vision along the edges. But this time there weren't any g-forces involved, and I had that instinctive certainty that I was very likely to pass out. So I triple-checked Good Old George [the automatic pilot], clicked the timer on my watch, and slid my seat as far back as it would go, knowing that if I passed out and fell forward on the control yoke, well, you know, that's pretty well assuring the bird would go into a dive that would take me straight into the sea. As a last thing to do I noted my time aloft since departure and what my position should be at that moment, and then, by God, I *did* pass out."

Hawke regained consciousness, as measured by his wristwatch and the clock on the instrument panel, just about one hour later. He had no idea where he was. He looked up and saw above him the contrail of a commercial jet high overhead. Hawke dialed in the international frequency to talk to the cockpit crew of the jetliner, established contact, and asked if they could tell him "just where in the bloody hell am I?"

The Aztec cruises for economical long-range flight at about 160 to 170 miles per hour. Hawke learned that in that hour, with calm weather conditions, he had traveled 400 miles to the north of where he had been when he slumped unconscious. He figured he should be off the coast of the Carolinas, so he swung into a wide left turn and headed due west. Sure enough; he made landfall along the North Carolina coast.

What had displaced Hawke's Aztec 400 miles north of

his previous position? He had been flying on a northeasterly heading for Bermuda, and now he was *due* north by those 400 miles. The Aztec could not possibly have flown that distance in the time figured.

Was this a phenomenon that more and more pilots were coming to accept as bilocation? It happened to John Hawke not once but twice. There were no witnesses, no proof, but no one flying who knew John Hawke ever doubted that everything happened precisely the way he described.

In the summer of 1992, John Hawke was lost forever. He was flying another Piper Aztec from France to Croatia/Yugoslavia when off the Italian coast, near Venice, a bomb exploded within one wing and sent the burning airplane plunging into the Adriatic Sea.

THE MYSTERY DEEPENS

Whirling magnetic compasses, nonfunctioning directional gyroscopes, and gyroscopic artificial horizons (attitude indicators) falling over uselessly, the sudden failure of electronic components, and the complete failure without any warning of all kinds of engines are not uncommon in the Bermuda Triangle. On most such occasions, the crews survive the moments of pure fright as an airplane suddenly seems to be getting away from its pilots. And it is possible to restart engines in flight; indeed, it's a common enough occurrence.

But that's no answer to these puzzling, frustrating, and sometimes lethal events. Flights like that of the Catalina through yellow murk, shared by so many other pilots (who never tell the press or anyone else save other pilots), are almost always accompanied by other failures and problems.

Obviously, something that tumbles gyroscopes, turns magnetic compasses into whirling dervishes, and makes hash out of the most advanced electronic systems in the world is a field of enormous power. The best explanation so far is that all these aircraft were enveloped by an intense electromagnetic field. The theory has its own problems because there are so many variables. Aircraft engines function on both electrical *and* electronic control systems, so why weren't the engines knocked out of service as well? There are alternators, generators, magnetos, wire leads, spark plugs, electronic monitoring devices, propeller synchronizers, "watchdog" leads for inlet and exhaust temperatures, manifold pressure gauges, carburetor temperature gauges, cylinder head temperature gauges, and oil pressure gauges. Why do some continue to function on some airplanes while their other systems die?

If the problems were caused by some form of static electricity, then the pilots likely would have encountered the effect known as St. Elmo's fire, familiar to pilots flying in thunderstorms or icy conditions, when accumulating static electricity causes blue and multicolored flames to dance along propeller blades, the nose, engines, and wings of an airplane, and even within the airplane cockpit and cabin, snapping and crackling and literally making hair stand on end and teeth ache from fillings charged by the electrical energy. The Catalina experienced none of these effects, nor did John Hawke.

WHERE DID THEY GO?

A list of all the ships known to have vanished while sailing through the waters of the Bermuda Triangle would fill many pages. And the mystery would be just as great. Just as there are many causes for airplanes to be lost without warning, such as engine failure, electrical systems failure, fuel tank explosions, sudden severe weather (such as a neutercane), collisions with other aircraft, and a host of other causes, so are there many reasons ships at sea go down and are never seen again.

There is a difference between a ship being lost and one that vanishes. Ships lost without proof means only that they have gone down without a specific known cause.

Dangerous cargos of volatile fuel can explode, for example, with such devastation that the ship is blown into chunks and no warning or distress signal is ever heard. Rogue waves and tidal waves have swamped even huge ships of ten thousand tons or more, and SOS signals were never sent out. Ships also collide, and if they explode or go down swiftly, they may do so without any radio signal or other sign. Storms take down dozens of seagoing vessels every year.

But other vanishing incidents occur that clearly cannot be explained in these ways. For example, *Rosalie* was a French vessel found drifting in the open sea on a voyage scheduled to enter port at Havana, Cuba. When the ship was reported missing, in 1840, a sea search was set in motion. The *Rosalie* was found, its condition excellent but its crew vanished into thin air except for a canary locked in its cage. The only clue as to how long the crew was gone was the canary—it was near starvation.

Bella, a schooner sailing the West Indies in 1854, was hailed by a passing ship. When no response was given, the ship closed with *Bella* and several men boarded the schooner. All hands were gone and the ship was in perfect condition.

The *James B. Chester* confounded its insurance company in 1855. Six hundred miles from the Azores, generally southwest, it was found and boarded by a search vessel. The report prepared by the captain of the boarding ship contained his judgment that for some unknown reason, the crew of the *Chester* either left their ship in great fear or were removed from the ship. All provisions were still aboard, all cargo was secured and accounted for, and every lifeboat hung properly in its davit. No human or animal remained on the ship.

Sailors around the world were convinced a ghost ship plied the ocean due west of the Azores in 1881. The mystery vessel was an unnamed schooner, which was hailed by the *Ellen Austin*. Again, no sign of life could be seen from the brig closing with the schooner. The ship was devoid of life, but this time a difference was recorded. The ship's log was gone, but in every other respect the vessel was in excellent condition. Claiming salvage, the captain of the *Ellen Austin* sent a crew to take the schooner to port. A storm blew up with huge waves and the two ships lost sight of one another. When the storm passed, the *Ellen Austin's* lookout spied the schooner. When they came together again, the *Ellen Austin's* crew discovered that the salvage crew was gone. Everyone had vanished. Another crew went aboard. In the darkness of the first night the ships separated. The schooner and its third and final crew vanished forever.

In 1921, the *Carroll A. Deering*, a beautiful five-masted schooner, closed with the shoreline at Cape Hatteras of North Carolina. Onlookers were surprised when the ship sailed directly against the shore and ran aground. People ran to the ship to help and climbed aboard. They were greeted by two cats—the only living creatures aboard the schooner.

By 1940, the rapid advancement of radio communications meant that a ship would never be isolated, especially when fairly close to land where other radio equipment was plentiful. Yet the mysteries of vanished crews continued. The *Gloria Colite*, its home port in Saint Vincent of the British West Indies, drifted aimlessly a few hundred miles south of Mobile, Alabama. With reports of the ship alerting the U.S. Coast Guard, the vessel was soon found, did not reply to hailing, and was boarded. The ship was in mint condition—except that not a human soul was to be found aboard.

By 1946 World War II was receding into memory, and advances in radios and electronics had transformed communications in another great stride forward. The inexplicable vanishings continued. The *City Belle*, a double-masted schooner 120 feet in length, sailing from the Dominican Republic to Providence in Nassau, put ashore in the Turks Islands. Sailors unloaded part of the cargo, twenty-two passengers boarded the ship, and it left the

Turks. A few hundred miles southeast of Miami, it was found drifting aimlessly. This time the lifeboats were gone, but the personal belongings of the crew and the passengers were untouched. No trace of anyone from the *City Belle* was ever found.

By 1969 the world was well into the space age, with orbiting satellites that could sweep the seas with high-resolution cameras, as well as aircraft that could fly at seventy to a hundred thousand feet with cameras that could pick out the number of people in a rowboat. One vessel, the *Vagabond*, drifted aimlessly—and lifeless—in the Atlantic. The *Cotopaxi*, a British cargo steamer, encountered a yacht making good headway but failing to answer hailing. Boarded by the British crew, the yacht was found to be guided by its automatic steering mechanism. No one was aboard. Close to Cape May in New Jersey, another crewless vessel, the *Teignmouth Electron*, drifted aimlessly.

Those people have never been found, and no one has ever come forth with an answer.

OUTCRY

No single event has inspired more hysteria, mystery, and a barrage of explanations ranging from interference from UFOs to other-dimensional seizures than the loss of five Grumman TBF Avenger torpedo bombers in the Bermuda Triangle in December 1945.

The case of the missing Avengers has inspired countless articles, books, television shows, and movies. Coming on the heels of World War II, when the news media was searching for "hot" stories, the disappearance of five torpedo bombers within close proximity of the U.S. mainland was made to order. It established the permanent legend of the Bermuda Triangle.

Because the case of the missing Avengers has occupied such a dominant position in the lore of vanished aircraft, a brief overview is in order. The five Avengers departed from Naval Air Station Fort Lauderdale in December 1945 at 2:10 P.M. on a normal training flight. They were to fly specific headings and maneuvers against "enemy targets." The training mission was scheduled to last for three hours—which would leave them well over two hours' worth of fuel to return to Lauderdale. Leading the mission was Lieutenant Charles Taylor.

Theories about the loss of the five torpedo bombers have yet to produce one single acceptable answer. These airplanes did not simply disappear. Their pilots became lost. We know this to be so because there were extensive conversations between the naval station in Florida and the Avengers, whose pilots were confused, apparently disoriented, bludgeoned by worsening weather—and confounded by magnetic compasses the pilots reported as spinning uselessly, although this latter problem seems to be missing from the greater majority of reports and stories.

The airplanes still had several hours of fuel time remaining when it became obvious that a problem was arising. Taylor, in fact, radioed to Lauderdale, his other pilots, and to anybody who was listening on an open frequency, "I don't know where we are. We must have got lost after that last turn."

With lowering clouds, strong winds, rain squalls, and diminished visibility, *and* Taylor's report that he believed his compass had become useless, confusion and disorientation was to be expected. In fact, two hours and thirty-five minutes after takeoff, Taylor was so shaken he reported by radio that the five Avengers were then over the Gulf of Mexico—a conclusion that caused great consternation in the naval station radio facilities trying to maintain contact with the bombers. Many studies and reenactments of the mission lead to the conclusion that it was virtually impossible for the Avengers to have flown from the islands east of Florida to the Gulf of Mexico.

By now hardly anyone on shore could understand why the five airplanes, with fourteen men, could be so confused. There was also great disagreement among the pilots in the airplanes as to where they were and what heading they should take to return to their station.

It was 4:45 P.M. when Taylor sent out his message that he was over the Gulf of Mexico. Radio contact was still being maintained with the formation, and fifteen minutes after Taylor's call, another pilot was heard clearly exclaiming, "Damn it, if we would just fly west, we would get home!"

His words failed to dissuade Taylor, who did *not* fly west. And within fifteen more minutes their fate was virtually sealed as a squall line rushed across the area, wiping out visibility for the five bombers.

Avengers were known to ditch into the ocean successfully on many occasions during the war. But this option had now gone for Taylor's group, plunged as they were into a storm with heavy rain, powerful winds, and turbulent seas. A ditching under those conditions was virtually suicide, and bailing out by parachute was hardly any better.

For another two hours intermittent radio contact was heard from the formation, the signals growing ever weaker—and then, when no fuel could have been left aboard those airplanes, all contact was lost. A massive search by hundreds of planes and ships never turned up so much as a single piece of wreckage from the lost squadron.

Certain elements should be considered to keep this case in perspective. During the war years when this area to the east of Florida was used for gunnery and bombing missions, it is estimated that several hundred aircraft were lost on those training flights. And among this number were more than one hundred other Avenger bombers, which reduces the "mystery" of the lost squadron to acceptable and understandable "normal possibilities."

Other losses of this type, because of the time period and the geographical location, never received a fraction of the attention and publicity that attended the missing five Avengers.

In 1945, during their return from a mission escorting

B-29 bombers striking Japan, twenty-one P-51 Mustang fighters encountered severe weather on their way back to Iwo Jima and vanished.

There wasn't a single newspaper story about the twenty-one lost fighter planes or the twenty-one young American pilots flying those fighters.

"SOME HUGE FORCE"

The incredible and harrowing misadventure that follows has been investigated as thoroughly as military security, and insistence on absolute anonymity, will allow.

It is one of the most revealing and frightening moments in the lives of men. There is no disappearance here, no vanishing airplane or ship or crew. In its quiet telling it evokes a sinister, disquieting fear. It leaves a haunting echo in the mind.

It has never before been told; it has never been published. This story is told in the very words of its source, without alteration.

First, you should know that I am retired from the United States Air Force, and logged 6,000 hours in basically three aircraft: the KB-50 [Superfortress aerial tanker], C-47, and the VC-131. I wish this narrative to be held in the strictest of confidence as even some of the crew members at the time were unaware of all the facts.

In 1960 I was flying a TAC [Tactical Air Command] KB-50 assigned to the 4505th Air Refueling Wing at Langley Air Force Base, and was en route from Lajes Air Base in the Azores to Langley with a short stop in Bermuda. After about seven hours into the flight the navigator announced that he had Bermuda on the radar and that we were about an hour out, which put us right on the money. After about fifteen or twenty minutes had gone by the nav motioned me to come back to his compartment and, when I arrived, he was quite concerned as we had, by the radar, at least, *stopped flying.* I too watched in disbelief as the image of the island did not move. We had been making a ground speed of perhaps 220 knots, but suddenly—*nothing!*

I quietly rechecked fuel with the flight engineer to make sure there were no problems. Our reserves were ample.

Returning to my seat I revised my ETA [estimated time of arrival] by thirty minutes, and then asked for updated winds aloft. The winds were as forecast. I then decided to descend as maybe we had gotten into the jetstream, and so we left 24,000 for 10,000 feet. At level-off I went into the nav compartment (wanting to stay off the interphone so as not to alarm the other crew members) and found that we were still 150–175 miles out with still no ground speed, at least by the radar. Ground radar was still unable to pick us up.

At that time I had not heard of the so-called Bermuda Triangle, though the term apparently existed. We had lost a KB-50 there in 1958 or 1959 when they got lost, ran out of fuel, and then ditched with the loss of one life. . . .

Now, I was really concerned. Perhaps a further descent would help, so I received clearance to about 6,000 feet and again revised my ETA by thirty minutes. A little while after leveling off, the nav motioned me back once again to his compartment. Now we were making some headway but still slower than what we should have been making.

When we finally landed, the navigator and I went into the weather station and talked to the head meteorologist. We told him the whole story and he showed us his winds aloft chart and where the jetstream was. The winds were as predicted and what we had used coming across and the jetstream was way north. He then laughed at us and refused to believe our story. My nav, who was the squadron nav and had much, much more overwater time than I, was humiliated as was I. We agreed not to share this incident with anyone because it was so preposterous we would be the laughingstock of the Wing. And even though we were more than an hour late arriving in Bermuda no one ever questioned us about it.

I don't believe in the supernatural and have never seen a UFO. But this incident made me feel like some huge force had me in its grip. It was very uncomfortable to watch the island of Bermuda become stationary on the radar.

This incident has never been shared with anyone else, not even my family, and I request this assurance of privacy. . . .

No one has ever been able to explain how a huge four-engined bomber could have been suspended in space for an hour.

11
"Nothing Will Help—He's Dead"

He drove carefully through the night on the rain-slick roads, handling his motorcycle with both skill and caution. When he saw the car swerving into the intersection before him he *knew* he'd hit it. The collision smashed his body. Bones cracked and broke like tenpins going down in bunches. When the medics finally got there, one said, "The best thing that could happen to this kid is that he'll die." A witness who'd been there looked at the medic. "He's been dead for a half-hour already."

But Ken Larson, with more than twenty smashed bones, not breathing, heart stopped, dead for thirty minutes, *heard the men talking about his death!*

This incredible tale would never have been published had there not been every opportunity to check the medical records of Cape Canaveral Hospital and the records of the paramedic teams and other emergency units of Cape Canaveral, Cocoa Beach, and Merritt Island, Florida, as well as the personal and official records and reports of Marine Patrol Officer and former Chief Detective Charles B. Autry of the Cocoa Beach Police Department, who had known William K. "Ken" Larson since the young man's childhood. This episode is a stunning testimony to the strength and ability of the human spirit to overcome the savaging of the physical body.

Where Ken Larson grew into a young man is important. From his home in Cocoa Beach, Florida, he watched great searchlights stabbing into the night sky as huge rockets were prepared for launch. His father, William

Frederick Larson, broadcast those launches on the ABC national television network, and when he returned home from work at night he thrilled the youngster with stories few youths are privileged to share. Often Ken would stand on the beach near the jetties of Port Canaveral so he could see the flaming giants fly off to other worlds. He met astronauts.

This vast enterprise of fire and dreams had a profound impact on the young man, for he was immersed in a world where the word *impossible* was banished. In his schoolbooks the idea of men walking on the moon was just silly fiction. Now he had met with and talked to the very same men who had kicked up moondust and bounded across that airless world. *Anything* was possible.

Through his father he met scientists, engineers, technicians, and other researchers who tried virtually anything that challenged them, including the challenge of the mind, where the goal was to develop mental skills that seemed just as fantastic as that "impossible" goal of walking on the moon.

"These people thrilled me," explains Ken Larson. "They kept saying that the greatest frontier to cross wasn't out in space. They would tap their heads and say, 'It's in here. Think of what we could do if we could use the power of the mind to accomplish *directly* what we do with our machines.'

"Those were the people who talked about mind over matter. They were trying to influence, to move, to shift different objects with *only* the power of the mind."

The elder Larson did investigative reports on research groups delving into psychokinesis, or telekinetics. They had set up laboratory conditions for their experiments, and Ken's father began taking the boy along with him to watch what was going on. The lab was made up of two rooms, separated by a thick glass wall. The experimenters sat in an anteroom. On the other side of the glass, on spindles of metal, plastic, and wood, were "targets" of paper, aluminum foil, shimmed brass, cardboard, and other materials. The room was sealed so there would be no movement of air to affect the targets.

Ken Larson watched these researchers concentrating, and the targets would begin to turn. As many as thirty would be turning at the same time, spinning in different directions. They invited Ken to give it a try. He didn't know at first if he was successful or not because the others could have been the motivating force.

Then Ken began to try on his own at home. Little by little he began to move targets when only he was present. He could do it!

"What's happening now," his father told him, watching him in his experiments, "could have a tremendous impact on our future lives. Think of it, Ken. You and those other people are turning or moving matter. If we can do this with inanimate objects, can't we do the same with biological cells and molecules?"

There was another, older friend who pushed Ken to try harder at everything he did. That was Chick Autry, chief of detectives, one of the top cops in town.

"Chick was a close friend of my father," Ken explains. "He was one of the truly honest people I've had the good fortune to know. There are so very few like him. But as well as I knew Chick when I was still in school, I *really* came to know him when I had my accident. That was in 1987. I came to have such tremendous faith in these people. They kept pushing back any horizons I had ahead of me.

"I began to understand the power of self-confidence and belief in what you're doing. I contracted pneumonia and my folks and my doctor wanted to put me into the hospital. I refused. If those guys could turn things with their minds, and I could do it a bit, then I could really concentrate and maybe affect my own body. Instead of going into the hospital I went to the local gym and went on a real binge of working out. I didn't feel very good and I hurt, but I kept at it, and the doctors were amazed—and so was I—because in a few days the pneumonia was gone. From that time on I swore that this is how I would take care of myself.

"Then there was this accident. . . ."

On June 20, 1987, Ken Larson was riding his motorcycle from Cocoa Beach to his job at Disney World in Orlando, where he worked the 11:00 P.M. to 7:00 A.M. shift. He drove west on the 520 Causeway in a light drizzle. It had rained the entire day and the roads were slick. Ken always dressed properly for a cycle trip: he wore a long-sleeved shirt, long pants, riding boots, heavy jacket, and a helmet. He had been riding motorcycles since he was nine years old, had ridden races on rough tracks, and was considered extremely competent on the bike.

He reached the intersection of the 520 Causeway and Tropical Trail on Merritt Island.

> There were several cars ahead of me, the light was green for me, some cars coming in the other direction, and a lady was turning left, heading north. As I approached the intersection I saw her starting her turn, and I said to myself, "Oh, no . . . don't let her turn, don't let her do something stupid. . . ."
>
> Just as my front tire got to the intersection, "something" told me, it was a feeling, almost like my own voice saying, "Brace yourself! She's going to turn!" That woman never saw me, she was concentrating on something else in her car, I couldn't avoid her. Just no way to prevent the impact I knew was going to happen. I was doing between 35 and 40 miles an hour, and I knew I was going to hit that car.
>
> I also knew I didn't want to impact that car head-on, that since I couldn't get out of this, I had to, I must, hit the car sideways. If I hit head-on I'd go over her car into oncoming traffic, or I'd hit her in such a way I'd go right through her back win-

dow. If you're thrown from a bike at this speed, mass and inertia plus the weight of the helmet means you have a 90 percent chance of dying from a broken neck. So I hit the front brakes and then hit the back brakes hard, I wanted to fishtail the bike into a sideways move. When I hit her car I was facing in the same direction as her car in the turn, but just before that the bike fishtailed the other way and now I was facing toward the back of her car.

I slammed into the side of her car with the right side of my body and the motorcycle slid underneath the car and, as I found out later, it skidded wildly another fifty feet beyond. I didn't care about the bike then, of course.

I don't really remember the impact. Later, trying to recall the sequence, it felt like only seconds later that I know I sat up, and I couldn't see anything. *I was blind.* I remember trying to breathe but couldn't get any air down my lungs. I wanted to try to beat on my chest to breathe but my arms wouldn't move. Then I could see, it was all a blur. I could hear things but I couldn't make out anything I was hearing. I was struggling so hard to breathe and then . . .

It was so strange. I didn't feel the blood moving through my body. It was strange even to think that, yet it was the clearest thought in my head. *I can't feel the blood moving through my body.*

I knew at that point that my heart had stopped.

It scared me half to death and I was trying to figure out how I was going to get my heart started again and how I was going to get air into my lungs. I couldn't do any of that. A few seconds later I was shaking uncontrollably, and I fell backwards from the sitting position on the ground.

I remember, "Oh, my God, I'm dying right here in the middle of this wet, cold road. . . . There's nobody around me that I love or who cares about me. . . ." Then I thought to myself, "Oh, Jesus, what is this going to do to Dad? And Nana, and Taylor, my son."

I didn't want to die and I tried hard to speak but I guess the words were in my head, and I was saying, or thinking, "Dear God, don't let me die here where I don't have anybody. . . ."

The next real recollection I have is waking up in the hospital. That was Cape Canaveral Hospital, and it was the next day. The first face I saw was Chick Autry, he was standing over me, and when I opened my eyes and looked at him, he sort of shifted his position so we locked eyes and he said, "My God, you idiot! What the hell do you think you're doing getting yourself on a motorcycle! What the hell is wrong with you?"

I remained quiet and Chick took my hand. Those powerful hands that could be so gentle. "You're going to be all right. You're here. We're taking care of you. You're all in one piece, you've got all your limbs, but man, you are busted up pretty bad. But never forget that we're going to make sure you're OK."

If it had been anybody else I was seeing through this wild tearing pain all through me, and the fact that I couldn't move my legs, I couldn't move my arms, I just didn't know what was going on, but I would never have believed anyone else at that moment. The way he held my hand, the way Chick looked into my eyes, and the way he spoke, well, I guessed tomorrow was going to come, after all.

Chick confirmed to me that my heart had actually stopped. That I had had no vital signs at all. *None.* "They lost you there for a while, son.

You were dead. Hear me? No two ways about it. You were deader than a doornail, but through some incredible work by those paramedics—to say nothing of the way you fought to live—they were able to bring you back through CPR and defibrillation."

He was quiet for a while and then he spoke again and there was nothing else in the world besides his voice. "There's a reason why you're here, why you came back. Why you're alive again. You better take a long, hard look at yourself and where you are and what you're doing with your life. Where you're going. You better figure out why the Man Upstairs is letting you live. *Again*," he emphasized. "You've got lots of time now to think about it, because nobody comes back unless there's a real good reason for it."

I thought of all the accidents and all the victims and all the dead people this man had seen through his years as a cop and I knew that he really knew where he was coming from.

I really didn't think I had anything like an out-of-body experience. Not at first. My whole world was confined to blinding pain and Chick's presence and voice. Then I had time to think and everything was dropping into place in my head.

I knew when my heart stopped. I remembered when my whole body just gave up its life. That was clear as a bell.

I did a lot of thinking the next five days. It was on the fifth day in the hospital that a gentleman walked into my room. He introduced himself, he was with another man. "Do you know who I am?" he asked.

I nodded. "Yes," I told him. "Your son died about a year and a half ago in a motorcycle accident. I was really sorry to hear about that."

He stared at me and turned pale and began

asking me questions about when his son died.
Especially how I knew about it. I didn't know
how; I just knew it. He told me there was no way
I could have known about the way his son died.
So I asked him why that was so important. He
said something about there had never been any
details given out about his son being killed. But
when I had my accident he and this other man
were talking about the time his own boy died.

"We were right there when you were lying
dead in the street," he said to me.

"No, that's not right," I told him. "I was
standing right next to you when you were talking
about it."

He acted as if someone had struck him.
"That's impossible," he said slowly. "You were
lying on the ground and we stood over you *and
you were dead.*" I couldn't make much sense out
of it all, and the older man patted my hand and
they left.

It made me think, and more pieces would be
fitting together about that highway scene. After I
got out of the hospital, and this is many weeks
later when I was going through therapy, I was
walking through the Merritt Square Mall and I
passed one of the security guards. I looked at him,
I knew who he was.

"Hi, Jerry," I sang out. "How you doing today?"

He looked at me strangely. "Where do you
know me from?" he asked. I couldn't place him,
we went through some small talk and I left.
About three months later I saw him again, and
this time he came right up to me. "Ken, did you
have an accident a year or so ago, on the 520
Causeway?" I nodded. "*Now* I know where I
know you from," he said quickly. "I was the first
officer at that accident scene. I was directing traf-

fic and I was there when the paramedics got to you."

I smiled. "Well, that answers where I know you from."

"No way," he said, shaking his head. "You couldn't have known me from that time. The paramedics were working on you the second they got there, and I was directing traffic, and you were dead, man. There was one time they got you going, a short time, I recall, but you were unconscious the whole time. You never even opened your eyes once."

"But . . ." I was stammering. "Jerry, I heard you talking to the medics! In fact, you talked to a paramedic named Tom."

He gave me a strange look, said, "See you later," and left me in one very big hurry. He seemed all shook up. I couldn't blame him. How could a dead man know who he was and also to whom he was talking, identified by name, when that dead man—myself—had *never seen* either of those people?

That is when things began to gnaw at me. The sense of *strange* became steadily stronger. Later, I discovered that this paramedic had his own mysteries to understand. He told me that when they were trying to restart my heart, and I was lying on the ground as dead as a long-landed fish, they told each other the only chance to bring me back was to get me to Wuesthoff Hospital in Cocoa.

This paramedic, and several others at the scene, much later confirmed to me that (1) I was dead, and (2) when I "heard" them talking about Wuesthoff, somehow the words came out of me. "No! Not Wuesthoff . . . got to go to Cape Canaveral Hospital."

The paramedic named Tom figured my heart

had started again. They checked me for vital signs and consciousness, stopped the CPR briefly, got out the stethoscope, and did a heart check on me. Tom looked up in amazement at the others. "Nothing! He's still as dead as he was!"

No one could understand how I could possibly have heard them and, even more baffling, how a dead man managed respiratory function and spoke to them. I didn't know either, not then, not now, but something had been driving through me, dead or alive, insisting on where I must be sent.

Again and again I've talked to the paramedics and others at the scene. Every one of them has said the same words. "You were dead."

The more I examined this incredible series of events, the clearer memories became. I cannot remember ever seeing a white light. I never saw my past life rushing by me in my mind. I didn't go through any tunnels. Not a bit of what I'd heard or read about with experiences involving near-death.

The mind has this wonderful, miraculous ability to help you forget things. Painful things, because if you remembered all the things you've gone through in your life, and all the hurt you've had, you'd be paralyzed and your body wouldn't work anymore, because it would fear what might continue to happen to you.

I remember with a searing intensity the pain I went through. But I can't *feel* it, and it's a memory instead of a pain. There's a difference. I go through short recollections, bits and pieces, of looking at myself and watching what was going on. That was the most startling of all.

I was able to look at myself lying in the road, dead. And it sure isn't all hearts and flowers.

Suddenly, I was recalling how, when all my

muscles let go and I had no muscle control left, I urinated involuntarily all over myself. And I was embarrassed! Then they cut away and removed all my clothes, and I was ashamed that I was lying naked in the road. But later, when I found out that this really *had* happened, I wasn't embarrassed at all—only during that time when I was dead and they were doing it, and I was watching it all *from above my body*, and I couldn't believe what was happening.

I learned, I guess, when I thought about it, that if you go, if you die and don't come back—or even if you do—you take with you the love and feelings of your life. I know the reason I fought so hard to regain my life and not to die, or to remain dead, because I was standing there and watching them fighting to get my heart started again, and I said to myself, it's been five years since I've seen my son. I can't leave him. He needs me and he's going to need me, and I can't leave this earth without ever getting to hold onto him again. These feelings definitely do go with you.

When the doctors first started coming to me in the hospital, I didn't understand much of what was going on. I was in so much pain, I was asleep or just passing out from the pain most of the time.

The doctors told me I had fractures up and down the right side of my body. Fractures of the leg. A couple of fractures of the thigh. Three fractures of the hip. Two fractures of the pelvis. Two fractures of the back. I had also partially dislocated my shoulder. I had broken seven ribs. I had also sustained a massive bruise, which created a deadly blood clot in my left leg.

Chick Autry was an incredible factor in getting my head straight. At least once every day, often more than that, Chick visited my room. He'd come in and tell me about some of the different breaks. He'd had three years of pre-med himself, and he'd draw pictures of the bone where it was broken. Each bone. And then he'd remind me that I had seen how the mind can move and affect visible objects at a distance and I could begin to do the same with my own body. Everything he did was aimed at helping me visualize how I could help my own broken bones draw back together *and heal.*

He said, at one point, the doctors had told him I wouldn't be able to move my legs. It could be many months before I'd have even the first tiny movement of my legs, my toes, or my feet. The doctors said it would be a very long time before I could make anything work. They also told Chick, and he told me right up front, that there was a very strong possibility that I would never walk again.

Chick held my eyes. "That's a lot of hogwash," he said angrily. "You'll walk again. *Believe that now and never stop believing it.* You just have to *want* to walk again, bad enough. You have to work at it. You *have* to do it. The doctors are wonderful people but they don't know everything. There are powers on this earth, and about this earth, and above this earth that none of us really understand. Just because we don't understand these things doesn't mean that they aren't there and that we can't use them. Visualize *inside* your body, son. Get inside there with your mind. *See* the breaks and start working in your mind to bring all the parts back together again. It *will* work. You've seen it done. You can do it too." I said I'd give it everything I had.

During the first few weeks in the hospital I'd be x-rayed every day, in the morning, with a special transport table. The table would slide out sideways and under the sheets I was on, and they'd lift me up and put me on this transport table. The pain was beyond belief. It was so excruciating that most of the time I'd pass out from the pain. It was devastating, but I went along with it.

After ten days in the hospital, one of the doctors came into my room carrying a stack of x-rays. He had the strangest look on his face. "The reason we've kept you lying flat, and not moving at all, is because of the traction we've had to keep you in. But, Good Lord, boy, *look at this*. . . ."

Then he showed me an x-ray of my abdominal section. "This is your abdomen," he said. "You see these organs over here, on the right side?" I nodded and he gave me a strange look. "Well, Ken, these should be over here on your *left* side. You've got enough space in there for an air conditioner!"

All my organs from my left side had compacted in a mass on the right side of my body.

Nurses came into my room several times each day to massage my stomach area, across the abdomen. And they did so very lightly, because almost any touch brought on waves of pain. The program I adopted with the doctors was that if I lay in a flat position on my back, with no more than a very thin pillow under my thighs, eventually all my organs *would move back* to the side of my body where they belonged!

Now, as all this went on, every moment I had I would concentrate on mentally affecting, moving, repairing my organs and bones. I tried to get into the frame of mind I recalled from the telekinetic experiments I had seen and in which I finally joined. Chick Autry hammered at me to keep doing that, to visualize my body responding to mental stimuli.

Something was working beautifully. Impossibly, according to several of the doctors, but beautifully. Slowly, steadily, my internal organs, which had been so violently displaced, were returning to where they belonged on the left side of my body. I never knew the impact I took when I slammed into that car had hurled everything over into a jumbled mass on my right side.

But the most telling sign that something more than hospital care was at work came through the incredible healing of my seven broken ribs. I was told these would take a very long time to heal, but after a few weeks in the hospital I was taken for a special examination down to the x-ray room. Everyone seemed to be excited about something, but I was like an outsider not permitted to share what they were buzzing about. Later that day they wheeled me back to x-ray. This time I insisted on knowing why I was taken back down again. "Not to worry," a nurse told me. "We've had a problem with the x-ray machine, but it's been checked out and it's working fine now."

Again they took a battery of x-rays and then returned me to my room. Several hours later one of the x-ray technicians came into the room. He studied me in silence for a while, then spoke softly. "We can't believe it. We just can't believe it." He kept repeating that until I broke in.

"What's the *problem?*" I wanted to know.

"Oh, there's no problem with the x-ray machine."

"Then what . . .?"

He gave me the strangest look, and suddenly he blurted out, *"All your ribs are completely healed."*

We stared at one another. Again he shook his head. "It just can't be! They're going crazy downstairs. All your ribs have healed completely, and I mean *perfectly*, in three weeks. In just *three weeks!*"

I sounded like a dummy. "What?"

"It can't be real," he went on. "But *it is*. Not only have your ribs healed completely, and like I said, perfectly, but there's no sign that they were ever broken. If we didn't have x-rays from before we could never tell you busted your ribs. Our x-ray machines can't pick up the first sign you ever so much as scratched a rib. Larson, right now your ribs are perfect." He shook his head again. "Three weeks!"

He pulled a chair next to my bed. "Look, busted ribs take a very long time to heal. They're notorious for that. You understand? If we weren't seeing this for ourselves, none of us would believe any of it." He studied me carefully. "You got anything special to tell me?"

I told him about the telekinetic stuff.

"You mean," he said slowly, "that you're affecting the healing mechanism of your body with your mind?"

"I don't know. I *guess* so."

He stood up. "Larson, that's the craziest thing I ever heard of. And I'll tell you what's even crazier, my friend. Whatever it is you're doing, *it works*. Don't stop." He grinned at me and left.

That *something special* was sure working. Other broken bones were knitting at a furious pace. I'd broken some twenty-three bones, and they hadn't put a single splint on me, and I was healing like crazy. The pain was still there, but so was the healing. Every moment I had to myself I kept concentrating on seeing inside my body, visualizing things coming together, healing, knitting, getting stronger. Sometimes I felt as if I had something like x-ray vision. And if I ever slacked off in working at the miracles that were happening to me, every day there was this tough cop glaring at me. Chick Autry never missed a day to visit me, giving me encouragement in between scathing growls to "stay with it."

The hospital was situated next to the ocean. Five weeks after my accident, when I was still a bone-smashed and helpless cripple, I got a few of the staff to help me into equipment that looked like something out of a bad science fiction movie. I had a brace on each knee, a brace across my back, a crutch under one arm and a surfboard under the other. I lurched and swayed my way to the beach, and I wobbled all the way down to the edge of the water. Right there I took off my braces and threw them up on the beach as far as I could. Then I'd strap the surfboard to my ankle. As I was sitting with my back to the ocean, I'd push up on my hands and with my hands slowly walk myself into the water until I got to the point where I could float. Then I crawled and squirmed my way onto the surfboard. All I could do then was to paddle about gently and I'm sure that through the pain, my grin must have been about as bright as that sun beating down on me.

Let me not mislead anyone. This was no fandango dance only five weeks after that crash on the highway. It hurt. I hurt so very badly I almost screamed with the pain. But I stuck with it. I knew I didn't want ever to be an invalid, and if I worked very hard at it myself and never let doubt rule my thoughts that I could get back into the excellent shape I was in before the accident.

Now, years later, often my back hurts. And my knees feel as if they'll hurt me all my life. Those bones and cartilage are really influenced by the weather. But, as I'd learned from a group of friends who had grinned in the face of the worst odds, including some tough combat, you always have your choice of the cup being half full or half empty. It is always a matter of choice. I'll say right now and for every day of the rest of my life that there's one thing much worse than waking up hurting. And that's waking up not feeling anything.

In that hospital, my bones were knitting at a furious pace. I kept up that head work too. I haven't the remotest idea of what telekinetics—TK—is, or how it works, and I'm not making any claims about anything, but there is that hard, inescapable reality of what went on in that hospital.

In the first days of my head clearing, so I could think, I was beginning to believe the doctors were right. I faced a year in that hospital. But everything was changing so fast! The knitting of my bones continued with that same "miraculous" speed the x-ray technician had told me about with my ribs, but now everything else was also knitting beautifully.

I never did spend a year in Cape Canaveral Hospital. It was *ten weeks*. The better I became the more time I spent in those head games, even in prayer and hard thinking—very hard. Instead of rolling along drearily with the pain I went along on that marvelous visualization, inside my body, and what could await me in the future.

I kept trying to understand this TK stuff, being able to affect my physical body with my mind. Any doubts I had vanished when I was told about my ribs being fully healed in so short a span of time. I had only to see the amazed expressions on the doctors and nurses to know how extraordinary my healing was. How, to them, so *impossible*. I didn't practice any particular routine beyond trying to visualize what I couldn't see—the cells of my body becoming healthier and stronger, the bones knitting, everything coming together. And when I weakened in resolve, as I did, I prayed. Did I ever pray! Not mumbling and murmuring, but way down deep as if I had a direct line to upstairs. I didn't expect answers, but I sure was pushing for results. Learning more about the body helped. I'd always thought of the skeleton as a collection of bones strung together on which you hung the human frame. I was amazed to discover that the bones are as much alive as any organ, and that every two years *all* the bones in the body are *new*. Boy, did that ever help! Knowing that the growing was just as much a part as the knitting seemed to accelerate the healing process.

And then . . . I was out of the hospital, walking. That's a laugh, really. It's tough to call the shambling gait I used to move along walking. But I got around on my own. I went on a strict physical therapy regimen at home. Exercising. Working with weights. Learning anew how to balance a body that more than once had become inert, dead tissue. So I wanted to *walk*? Well, I had to teach myself to walk all over again. *I didn't know how to walk anymore.* I still had to find my sense of balance, which somehow seemed just beyond my reach.

At the same time, I was so sensitive to myself that by now I could sense or feel what was going on inside me. I was amazed that I still had musculature, since my muscles didn't know how to work on the autonomic basis I had just taken for granted. It was both difficult and fascinating to realize I was teaching my brain and my muscles how to work together in the coordination you need for autonomic functioning so that I wouldn't have to prethink every motion, and instead of stumbling about like a poorly built robot, I could move and walk and twist as second nature.

I also wanted to work. I decided to try the-

ater, as I had once before, and I went to the Surfside Playhouse to audition for a part in *Harvey*.
At the time I was still walking with a cane and a
crutch, and I put aside the crutch and walked up
onto the stage with just the cane. They looked
strangely at me.

"Man, how can you possibly do a show?" the
director asked. "You're a physical wreck. I don't
mean to be unkind, but . . ." He left the rest un-
said.

"You give me the part," I told him, "and I
promise you that six weeks from now that crutch
and this cane will be *gone*, and I'll walk and work
without them and I'll do the part."

I got the part. Six weeks later I walked onto
that same stage without the crutch or the cane.

Whatever this "test" was I was going
through, of self, or life, I do not know, but the
squeeze wasn't yet over. In 1988 I returned to
work. Everything, despite the pain and some en-
during problems with physical movement, was
coming up roses. I had not only survived that
smashup but had died and in a sense been reborn.

Then in February 1989 the world caved in on
me again. I was at work when a piece of heavy
equipment was dropped onto my hand. Several
hundred pounds smashing into your hand usually
means that for all intents and purposes the rest of
your life is spent with one useful hand and one
clumsy appendage. When the accident happened a
fellow worker tried to lift the metal container off
me. He couldn't budge it, yelled for help, and it
took four guys just to free me where I was
pinned.

Two of the fingers on my right hand were
absolutely crushed. The skin had split like ripe
melon dropped from a high roof. The tissue inside
had spurted out like some pulpy, bloody fruit.

Back I went to the hospital, where the first inclination of the doctors was to amputate the fingers—right away. I couldn't blame them but I refused. I pleaded and I begged and I cajoled the doctors into doing everything they could short of amputation. I knew the route back to healing and I wasn't ever going to forget it. The doctors worked on me and when they were through my hand was bandaged up. They sent me home and told me to return in a few weeks. They didn't leave much doubt that they would amputate then.

I didn't keep those bandages on for those weeks. Every day I'd take off the bandages and clean the wounds and use my own salve with vitamin E oil and aloe and triple ointments and all sorts of good things, and then wrap up the hand again. I couldn't work, so I spent much of my time sitting at home, leaning back in a reclining chair, my eyes closed, and I would visualize those fingers healing themselves. Molecules and cells, all swirling to come together and *heal*. I could "see" my fingers shifting the smashed pulp back into healthy tissue.

When I returned to the hospital the talk again was of amputation. But now it was *partial* amputation, because the tissue atop my fingers was all dead and of no use. Again I refused. I continued my own therapy and spent almost every waking moment trying to turn flesh and bone into something that was *growing* back to normal.

Ten weeks to the day after the accident, at the Space Coast Orthopedic Center, a doctor removed all the clumsy home wrappings. He stared at my fingers, his eyes wide. He didn't say a word to me, but called in a small crowd of doctors and other medical personnel.

The sounds of disbelief and the mixed exclamations were orchestral music to me. The tissue that had been squeezed out of the fingers, and that was dead, had somehow gone back into the fingers where they rejuvenated! Now the fingers were perfectly healthy, functioning tissue, and the skin had closed up smoothly.

Today I have full use of those fingers. Two of them are a bit flatter and a little wider than the others, but through the use of my mind and continued self-therapy, they are fully functional.

Some months later, working at Surfside Playhouse, I met the girlfriend of one of the actors. It was a case of synchronicity, or whatever they call amazing coincidence. The night of my highway smashup she was in a car only four cars behind the intersection where I'd crashed. She saw the whole thing, and had described to her friends, shaking and upset, how she'd seen this young man killed, and watched his body being driven away in an ambulance.

She kept staring at me, her eyes wider and wider, and she turned pale. "It can't be . . . it just can't be," she kept repeating. "I saw you killed. *I saw you dead!* I was standing right over you, you had no heartbeat, you weren't breathing, you were DEAD, and then they took your body with them. . . ." Her voice broke and she coughed into silence. Daphne, who had been there without my knowledge, had several other friends who had also seen the accident. Again, that coincidence. They lived close by some of the paramedics. Long after I left the hospital, I was in Cape Canaveral and I saw several of these people outside their home, and suddenly I recognized one of them, and I said, "Hey, Tom! You're Tom, right? Man, I want to thank you. You saved my life!"

"When?" He looked at me like I was crazy.

I told him about the accident and the CPR and everything else, and he turned white. It was *him!* The man who did everything he could to save my life on that wet road that night. A man I had never seen with my eyes before, but whom I recognized immediately.

My life is *so* different now. I don't have the fear of death I had when I was younger. After all, I'm living on the gift of borrowed time, so what's to fear? I was given the greatest second chance there is and I'm going to make the most of it.

I learned from several very close friends who've lived their lives without ever giving up, no matter what the odds. They had a tremendous influence on me. In a sense this is being superhuman. Not physically but in the mind and in the heart and the abilities we have and those to be developed to achieve the "impossible."

What I was taught about using my mind to go deep into my own body, well, it carried me along and I absolutely had to believe in it, and every day in that hospital Chick Autry would remind me of what was being done, what *I* could do, with this TK ability, that if I believed strong enough I could repair myself.

"By God, you *can* do it!" he would pound at me at the end of every visit. And he told me of other people and what they had been through and they used this "TK insight" to refuse to allow them to be crippled or destroyed. These were people who had been blind and regained their sight. A man who'd broken his neck twice and was told he'd be a paraplegic and he laughed at the doctors and a month later, they were shocked when they saw the x-rays that showed where the breaks had healed.

The rule was, "If it doesn't kill you, you can make it serve to make you stronger."

I had help, love, praying, strength from my friends and family. I will be forever grateful to all of them.

Because I'm alive and better than I was before I died.